The Archaeology of Prostitution and Clandestine Pursuits

The American Experience in Archaeological Perspective

UNIVERSITY PRESS OF FLORIDA

Florida A&M University, Tallahassee
Florida Atlantic University, Boca Raton
Florida Gulf Coast University, Ft. Myers
Florida International University, Miami
Florida State University, Tallahassee
New College of Florida, Sarasota
University of Central Florida, Orlando
University of Florida, Gainesville
University of North Florida, Jacksonville
University of South Florida, Tampa
University of West Florida, Pensacola

THE ARCHAEOLOGY OF

Prostitution and Clandestine Pursuits

Rebecca Yamin and Donna J. Seifert

FOREWORD BY MICHAEL S. NASSANEY

UNIVERSITY PRESS OF FLORIDA

Gainesville / Tallahassee / Tampa / Boca Raton

Pensacola / Orlando / Miami / Jacksonville / Ft. Myers / Sarasota

First cloth printing, 2019
First paperback printing, 2023

28 27 26 25 24 23   6 5 4 3 2 1

Library of Congress Cataloging-in-Publication Data
Names: Yamin, Rebecca, 1942– author. | Seifert, Donna J., author. | Nassaney,
    Michael S., author of foreword.
Title: The archaeology of prostitution and clandestine pursuits / Rebecca
    Yamin and Donna J. Seifert ; foreword by Michael S. Nassaney.
Other titles: American experience in archaeological perspective.
Description: Gainesville : University Press of Florida, 2019. | Series:
    American experience in archaeological perspective | Includes
    bibliographical references and index.
Identifiers: LCCN 2018054713 | ISBN 9780813056456 (cloth) |
    ISBN 9780813080017 (pbk.)
Subjects: LCSH: Prostitution—United States—History. | Brothels—United
    States—History. | Social archaeology—United States.
Classification: LCC HQ144 .Y36 2019 | DDC 306.740973—dc23
LC record available at https://lccn.loc.gov/2018054713

The University Press of Florida is the scholarly publishing agency for the State
University System of Florida, comprising Florida A&M University, Florida
Atlantic University, Florida Gulf Coast University, Florida International
University, Florida State University, New College of Florida, University
of Central Florida, University of Florida, University of North Florida,
University of South Florida, and University of West Florida.

University Press of Florida
2046 NE Waldo Road
Suite 2100
Gainesville, FL 32609
http://upress.ufl.edu

Contents

Figures

Foreword

So many aspects of our lives are hidden—our deepest desires, our financial assets, the scars we carry from childhood, and the objects that comfort us in private spaces, to name just a few. Some may bring social disapproval, so we conduct them covertly, perhaps with reticence, embarrassment, and risk. Social science inquiry is premised on the privileges of scholars to interrogate and infiltrate the lives of others to understand how they negotiate their social positions and enact their will in the face of incalculable cultural, economic, and political constraints. Life experiences entail a dialectic of action occurring at conscious and unconscious levels, such that interviews and documentary sources alone cannot reveal the full range of behaviors that people engage in and the motivations for their choices.

The detritus left in the wake of these activities, in concert with oral and textual accounts, is grist for the archaeological mill. By examining the materiality of people's lives, historical archaeologists become privy to what makers, users, and discarders may have thought to be trivial, inconsequential, and insignificant. Indeed, syringes, buttons, mutilated dolls, bent pins, perforated coins, and alcohol bottles are indices of desires, aspirations, and lived experiences. Suffice it to say that the constructed past has lessons to teach us, as we juxtapose what we learn from these small things forgotten with the ways we understand ourselves. The study of the past brings into focus our lives and those of others who are seemingly very different from us. These likenesses and divergences illuminate our present purpose and the historical practices that were foundational in the American experience.

Most historical archaeology evidence points to conformity—the large-scale patterns of subsistence, settlement, consumer choices, and other mundane traces that people discarded in the course of their often prosaic lives. In contrast, instances of rebellion to social mores and secretive activities are so fascinating that they often attract considerable public interest. Some 30 million anxious television viewers in 1986 watched as Geraldo Rivera opened Al Capone's vault in Chicago's Lexington Hotel, only to be disappointed by the recovery of a few empty liquor bottles. Other more strictly archaeological examples abound. In Menlo Park, New Jersey, archaeologists discovered Thomas Edison's hidden vault, where he curated documents related to his experimental discoveries. In 1991 I was invited to locate what we would now call a "time capsule" buried by the Class of 1878 beneath a ceremonially planted tree on the campus of the University of Massachusetts. A tantalizing description of "a box containing documents of great importance to future ages" motivated our search, leading to the discovery of a rather unremarkable and partially damaged copper box. We soon learned that its wet contents were duplicated in the university library, though the commemorative act was central to the students' collective experience. And finally, we were initially perplexed by the recovery of a series of linked, pointed wires from the eighteenth-century site of Fort St. Joseph until we noted its surprising similarity to comparable specimens, most notably the cilice worn by Silas, a devout monk, in Dan Brown's *The Da Vinci Code*. Likely employed discreetly to emulate the suffering of Christ and attain a state of grace by one of the denizens of the fort, it implies the deep religious piety of a Catholic practitioner on the frontier of New France. These places and objects provided archaeologists an entry into the mind-sets of people in the past who sought to gain command of a world that appeared to be beyond their control.

Few personal acts attract more interest and curiosity than the intimacies associated with prostitution. Known figuratively as "the world's oldest profession," the sale of sexual favors is a type of commercial activity that still occupies an ambiguous legal and moral place in society. Americans have disparaged prostitutes, their clients, and their promiscuous liaisons while recognizing the persistence of these practices among people of varying ethnicities, racialized groups, religions, and classes. Scholars have attempted to penetrate the inner recesses of these acts to understand the motivations that compelled women (and less so, men and other sexualities) to commodify their bodies for economic survival.

In *The Archaeology of Prostitution and Clandestine Pursuits*, Rebecca Yamin and Donna J. Seifert highlight one of the major achievements of historical archaeology—the recognition of the capacity of people without conventional forms of social and economic power to attempt to control their own lives, express themselves, and defy the constraints placed upon them. In the parlance of agency theory, people may not have "power over," yet they still have "power to." Yamin and Seifert view agency—the ability of people to enact decisions in their lives in the face of the structures that constrain their possibilities of realizing their true selves—as the central premise that links the lives of prostitutes, freedom seekers, children, the working class, and Chinese immigrants, to name just a few of the subaltern groups explored in this book.

As the authors note, sometimes agency posed risks. Self-liberated African Americans fleeing bondage in the American South needed self-reliance and trust in a host of strangers. They faced the real possibility that they could be caught and returned to the plantation, where enslavers meted out harsh punishments to deter further defiance. Similarly, a woman's name and her virtue were despoiled by engaging in what some considered promiscuous sex, as were the reputations of madams, pimps, and johns, though perhaps to a lesser degree for male participants, pointing to the hypocrisy of attitudes regarding sex work.

The authors emphasize that the clandestine activities they discuss were not always hidden; however, they all display agency in opposition to accepted norms of behavior. People of all walks of life sought to define themselves on their own terms and challenge social and cultural stereotypes. For example, working women who were impudent and sociable, rather than timid and retiring, were considered a threat to a society that revered the idea that a woman's place was in the home. For the working class, prostitution was not a disgraceful profession, as it was often understood as an economic necessity in a cultural context that was communal, raucous, antipatriarchal, and considerably more relaxed about sex than was bourgeois culture.

The greatest predictor of prostitution was not ethnicity, birthplace, or even class, but rather the death of a parent, especially the father. How this correlates with the timing of initial consensual or coerced sexual relations remains unknown, though many women were often introduced to sex early on within their own communities and did not have prudish values about using it to earn a living. What is clear is that nineteenth-century working-class women did not make a living wage in urban or rural settings; they were generally paid half as much as men. A single female resident in a brothel could make ten times more than her sister fulfilling a traditional role. Independence from men also emerges as a theme in the writings of prostitutes. They engaged in prostitution to have the finer things in life, such as fancy clothing. Despite the hardships of this work, it was a lucrative endeavor—so long as one was deemed physically desirable.

Expectedly, the places where these sexual acts took place often left signa-tures that express both the splendor and tribulations of this lifestyle. Indeed, the artifacts and their contexts, both public and private, allow us to construct a much more nuanced picture of what daily life was like for the women who made their living in commercial sex. Grooming artifacts such as skin creams, hair-care products, scented face powder, and rouge were used to enhance beauty and promote a youthful appearance in keeping with the theatrical na-ture of the profession. Similarly, the recovery of perfume and cologne bottles, cream jars, tooth-powder jars, toothbrushes, hair brushes, combs, soap dishes, pitchers, and washbasins reflect the importance of physical attractiveness in the parlor house. Because prostitutes were constantly exposed to an array of communicable diseases, they used alcohol, morphine, opium, and other drugs to treat pain. Collections recovered from brothels include about twice as many pharmaceutical items as found in saloons. Brothel assemblages generally have larger proportions of clothing artifacts, testifying to the frequent ritual of un-dressing and dressing. Ceramics and food remains are indicative of the dining practices that characterized these places. While both men and women con-sumed foods in this social context, what they ate and how it was served dif-fered. The remains associated with eating and drinking suggest two levels of consumption indicative of the "front-stage" and "backstage" behaviors of cli-ents and residents respectively. Different classes of brothels also exhibited no-table variation. Nearly all brothels displayed evidence of alcohol consumption (perhaps to lower inhibitions and anesthetize the women); however, cham-pagne was preferred by the clientele of the most expensive establishments, along with fancy dishes, choice cuts of meat, and exotic foods.

While prostitution was a defining characteristic of truly urban nineteenth-century cities, it also existed in more rural areas. In fact, wherever transient working-class men congregated, the sex trade followed. Studies conducted in railroad camps, mining camps, western towns, and elsewhere disclose the am-biguous attitudes pertaining to the sale of sexual services. It was both present and illegal in many places, such as in Fargo, North Dakota, where the city benefited financially from informal regulation of illicit businesses by fining practitioners of the sex trade. Hence, prostitution is deeply woven into the fabric of the American experience.

Historical archaeologists are well positioned to examine the motivations and consequences of behaviors associated with prostitution and other clan-destine pursuits. As the authors note, archaeological evidence reveals agency where agency was not always obvious and lets us see what is, at the very least, unconventional, and often courageous behavior. They discuss how drinking on the job was a form of workplace resistance to the impersonal forces of the capitalist economy, as also attested by the discarded cutlery wasters tossed out the window of the Russell Cutlery in defiance of the boss. Archaeological approaches involving excavation and mapping can add immeasurably to an understanding of how the Underground Railroad really worked—how people moved invisibly through the landscape and who guided them. Objects concealed in the walls and other domestic spaces by Americans of many different backgrounds demonstrate continued efforts to seek protection and ward off evil in their New World homes. The study of spaces inhabited by the enslaved has illuminated various clandestine practices associated with resisting power and maintaining personal agency. The integration of wives and families in frontier settlements prompted the segregation of districts for prostitution and other transgressions, either by statute or by custom.

Evidence of undesirable behaviors (to some) is rapidly being erased from the landscape and excluded from dominant narratives. When I first visited Alameda Street in Los Angeles in 1974, it appeared as a gentrified, commercial center catering to tourists and their families by offering ethnic foods and souvenirs. I had no idea that a century earlier prostitution was concentrated in this area by law. Archaeology can help us identify, investigate, and understand the past as different from the present. Archaeologists must be vigilant in recovering and interpreting sexuality and secretive behaviors from the past in ways that do justice to those who preceded us and to avoid moralizing about their behaviors from our own lofty perch, fully recognizing the complexity of the archaeological record. For example, prostitutes played important roles in civilizing towns of the West by providing and organizing social welfare services, medical care, and community events. Prostitutes in the mining West were working women whose labor supported themselves and supported the labor of others. They participated in the expansion of the world system and contributed to the formation, development, stability, and identity of the West. We are well served to consider and remember how material indications of class were manipulated in brothels, the limitations placed on gender roles for women in the nineteenth century, and how women countered these conditions. Archaeology suggests inherent contradictions in brothel life, perhaps its most distinctive trait.

In closing, the authors reflect on the role of anthropologists: should they merely observe and record, or interpret and pass judgment? Is sex work inherently immoral and demeaning or a means of controlling one's own body to make a living? As more anthropologists aim to contribute to the critical and activist tradition of the discipline, they cease to be mere witnesses of the human condition and strive to change contemporary society informed by lessons inherited from the past. The implications are wide ranging. Prostitution dehumanizes women *and* men by reducing them to caricatures. It also serves to maintain patriarchy, much in the same way that a woman may experience demands for sexual services if she wants to keep her job. Gender politics arguably changed with the onset of the women's movement in the 1970s; however, women still struggle for control over their bodies, access to STEM education, and equal pay. The struggles take many forms, both public and private, in the hidden and explicit material acts aimed to transform the American experience and our nation into a more perfect union.

Michael S. Nassaney
Series Editor

Acknowledgments

Each of us managed a cultural-resources project on the site of a brothel. By necessity, we dove into the history and archaeology of brothels and the lives of the prostitutes who occupied them. This research led us to conversations with other colleagues who were also exploring the underside of history, and we are grateful for their new perspectives and stimulating ideas. Scholars who have shared their research and interpretations include Pam Crabtree, Kristen Fellows, Kristin Gensmer, Alexander Keim, AnneMarie Kooistra, Jade Luiz, Claudia Milne, Anna Munns, Jennifer Porter-Lupu, Angela Smith, Mary Van Buren, and Mark Warner, and we hope we have done their work justice here. Rebecca would also like to thank Katrina Eichner, Amanda Johnson, Andrea Kozub, and Ashley Morton for their interesting ideas about brothels and personal hygiene. Much of that work is discussed in chapter 2, and without it the book would be considerably less up-to-date.

Our own work on the archaeology of prostitution began with large urban data-recovery projects done when we were employees of John Milner Associates, Inc. (JMA), Donna in the firm's Alexandria office, and Rebecca in the firm's Philadelphia office in the 1990s. We are grateful to Charles Cheek and Dan Roberts for giving us the opportunity to do those projects and to JMA employees Julie Cruz, V. Casey Gonzalez, Sarah Ruch, Margy Schoettle, and Rob Schultz for supporting our efforts. Rebecca's work on the brothel at Five Points was done in the context of the Foley Square project. Members of the Foley Square/Five Points staff who contributed to the brothel analysis included Michael Bonasera, Steve Brighton, Lauren Cook, Pam Crabtree, Tom Crist, Heather Griggs, Claudia Milne, and Paul Reckner. The Washington, DC, project teams included Elizabeth Abel, Jo Balicki, Charles Goode, Dana Heck, Elizabeth Barthold O'Brien, and Margarita Jerabek Wuellner. Their expert analyses of historic sources, ceramics, glassware, faunal remains, human remains, sewing materials, historic images, and clay pipes made it possible to see our brothels from the inside. We are grateful to them all.

The inclusion of "clandestine pursuits" was not our idea. Michael Nassaney, the series editor, originally suggested we consider other illegal activities, but since prostitution wasn't always illegal, we had to broaden the title. Using the concept of agency to link prostitution with these other pursuits was our idea and proved to be stimulating in itself. As discussed in the book, so much of historical archaeology is about conformity that it is a relief to be able to focus on nonconformity, and it is in this sense that we employ the concept of agency. Many colleagues were prodded for ideas about which clandestine pursuits to include, and we thank them even though we aren't even going to try to list them all. Michael Nassaney, however, stands out, and we are grateful to him for both inviting us to write this book in the first place and for feeding us good ideas along the way. We are also grateful to him for his comments on a first draft of this manuscript and to Deborah Rotman for her extensive and constructive comments on the same. It is invaluable to receive such detailed comments, and we only hope we have done them justice. And we thank Meredith Morris-Babb, director of the University Press of Florida, and her assistant Lilly Dunaj for guiding us through the process of making a manuscript into a book. Thanks also to Eleanor Deumens, the press's excellent in-house editor, and to Lisa Williams for her careful copy edit.

New research for the book was conducted in the archives of the Van Pelt Library at the University of Pennsylvania, at the New York Historical Society in New York City, and at the Catherine McElvain Library of the School for Advanced Research, Santa Fe. Donna extends special thanks to Laura Holt, SAR librarian, for invaluable assistance in finding and acquiring digital sources and books through interlibrary loan. Cheryl Foote shared many of her own books on the history of women in the West. She also offered persistent moral support and delightful distraction on New Mexico historic foodways as we each struggled to stay focused on our respective writing projects. Mark Warner provided the digital copies of the Sandpoint reports and facilitated contacts with the Bonner County Historical Society, which generously provided the print of the historic photograph of the Sandpoint Restricted District. Kelly Dyson and her team at the Library of Congress Duplication Services assisted in the acquisition of the digital images of the Boschke map and Sachse print. Kristen Fellows,

Kristin Gensmer, Anna Munns, Angela Smith, and Mary Van Buren generously gave permission to quote from and cite their papers while in manuscript.

Our personal libraries provided some of the oldest sources of inspiration, for instance, *La Vida* (1965) by Oscar Lewis and *The Primitive World and Its Transformations* (1953) by Robert Redfield, while the relatively recent book, *Paid For: My Journey through Prostitution*, about the experiences of an Irish prostitute in the 1990s (Moran 2013) provided an insider's view of the contemporary practice of prostitution. Lauren Cook suggested Moran's book, and we appreciate his understanding of the complexity of the subject. In addition to Lauren, many other colleagues and friends acted as sounding boards and protectors from error. Rebecca is particularly grateful to Julia Costello and Mary Beaudry in this capacity. Dawn Thomas, as always, provided a helping hand when needed and moral support throughout the process. Donna had the last-minute good luck of finding an article in a college alumni magazine about a 2017 collection of articles on street-based sex work. In the collection she found Daniel J. Steele's paper giving us the cop's-eye view of commercial sex to complement Moran's insider's view.

The Washington, DC, work benefited from the contributions of many colleagues, who informed our understanding of foodways and historic land use, including Cheryl Holt, Lisa O'Steen, and Leslie Raymer (floral and faunal analyses); Gerald Kelso (pollen analysis); and Irwin Rovner (phytolith analysis). The investigations in Hooker's Division (modern Federal Triangle) were sponsored by the Pennsylvania Avenue Development Corporations, and the investigations of Mary Ann Hall's house on the Island (the modern National Mall) were sponsored by the Smithsonian Institution. Justin Estoque of the Smithsonian's Office of the Physical Plant facilitated every step for us during our Mall excavations. Donna extends an extra-special thanks to Justin for taking her to the second-floor, east-facing window in the new National Museum of the American Indian on the Mall—before the museum opened—so she could see the view from Mary Ann Hall's brothel to the U.S. Capitol. James O. Hall shared key information on Ellen Starr and her connections in Hooker's Division and with the Lincoln assassination. Joseph Scheele wrote and called Donna in 1989 to tell her about his boyhood experience in one of Hooker's Division's brothels, when he was about 13 years old, just before passage of the Kenyon Act in 1913, which closed the Division. Donna also heard from a descendent of the Shea family who shared the family version of how Maria Shea came to shoot a cop on her doorstep in 1871. She thanks them both for contacting her.

We also want to thank the following for making pictures available from their collections: Richard Veit, Mark Leone, Jade Luiz, Mary Beaudry, Mary Praetzellis, Ian Burrow, Patrick Harshbarger, Bill Liebeknecht, the Onondaga Historical Society, and John Milner Associates, Inc. (now Commonwealth Heritage Group, Inc.).

Family and friends have put up with a lot of complaining about this project, and we thank them for their forbearance. In spirit—if not in print—we dedicate the book to the late Dan Roberts, who was director of the cultural resource division of John Milner Associates, Inc., when we began the New York and Washington, DC, projects. We know that Dan would have supported this effort to the end. The thing that was special about Dan was that he encouraged scholarly work over and above what is required for contract archaeology, which is, alas, rare. Our projects were mandated by public law and supported with public funds. Following Dan's lead, we are committed to producing work that contributes to scholarship and is accessible to the interested nonspecialist.

1

Agency and the Archaeology
of the Unconventional

It is the great advantage of archaeology that we get to look at what is hidden, that is, discarded objects never meant to be examined by anyone, certainly not scholars. The archaeology of prostitution and clandestine pursuits has a special place in this endeavor. Unlike the remains of everyday activities—the usual stuff of historical archaeology—the remains of clandestine activities were supposed to be hidden even when they were in use. This makes them particularly fascinating, especially the ones that are connected to sex. Both of us have worked on projects that included brothels, and both of us have noticed that of all the things we talk about, people (scholars and laypeople alike) are most interested in the evidence of prostitution.

Why does the archaeology of prostitution matter? Is it any less important than the archaeology of farmsteads, cities, industry, or battlefields? It matters because prostitution is a singular type of commercial activity occupying an ambiguous legal and moral place in society. It is part of culture history, labor history, and gender history. It is generally considered immoral—as well as exploitive—and the huge advantage of using archaeological data to approach the subject is its undeniable materiality. Artifact assemblages associated with brothels are more complicated than the generalized portrait of brothels in nineteenth-century written accounts (for example, Sanger 1939, originally published 1858) or even more recent feminist studies (for example, Hill 1993; Stansell 1987; Walkowitz 1982). The artifacts and their contexts, both public and private, allow us to construct a much more complex picture of what daily life was like for the women who made their living in commercial sex.

Until relatively recently women were missing from archaeological discussions of the past. It took a good deal of interpretive effort and refocus to find them, a task that, thankfully, has been realized (for example, Gero and Conkey 1991; Rotman 2015; Wall 1994). In this book, women are the main players, but there are others: railroad workers and factory workers, prisoners and soldiers, smugglers and pirates. There are also grownups who hid things in their houses or yards to deal with the insecurities of life and children who hid things just for the fun of it. While some of the clandestine activities that will be discussed here were not totally hidden, they all have one thing in common: they display agency in opposition to accepted norms of behavior, in some cases to the law and in all cases to playing it safe in spite of various constraints. We seem to love watching others break the rules, break the law, break out of the constraints that guide our lives. Whether it includes sex or not, there is something irresistibly interesting about taking chances—being unconventional.

Finding the Evidence

Although there was some interest in the possibility of an archaeology of prostitution in the 1980s (Simmons 1989; Wegars 1989) and even as early as 1972 (Baker), it was large urban projects of the 1980s and 1990s, done in compliance with cultural resource laws, that produced an American archaeology of prostitution. Plenty of archaeological investigations of prostitution had been done elsewhere in the world—Pompeii in Italy is the most famous example—but we did not have large enough assemblages of artifacts or structural remains associated with brothels in the United States to begin an archaeological analysis of brothel life. It was the huge urban projects on construction sites that made it possible (see Rothschild and Wall 2014 for a general discussion of urban archaeology).

Section 106 of the National Historic Preservation Act (NHPA), passed in 1966, requires federal agencies to take into account the effects of their actions on historic properties (King 2005:89). Compliance with Section 106 calls for a multiphased evaluation process for properties that will be disturbed by proposed construction or any kind of ground-disturbing activities, either on federal property or through federally funded or permitted projects. The evaluation process includes tracing the history and prehistory of the place that will be affected; determining whether there might be something left in the ground relating to that history and/or prehistory; figuring out if whatever is there is still intact and worth investigating; and planning for its excavation if avoidance is not possible. Because projects done in compliance with this law are initiated by pending ground disturbance rather than academic research agendas, they have a particularly high potential to encounter unanticipated evidence of the past.

These expensive urban projects have opened up areas for research that were neither accessible nor affordable before. This is especially true in cities where parking lots—the only land left for development—have become construction sites. The foundations of nineteenth-century buildings, taken down years before to make room for cars, are often hidden below the paved lots. Those buildings had displaced earlier ones, and their basement floors often covered former backyards where privies, cisterns, and wells—all of which urban archaeologists call "features"—were located (Figure 1.1). Although

Figure 1.1. Overhead photograph of foundations and features uncovered on the Courthouse site at Foley Square in Lower Manhattan, New York City, 1991. Photograph by Dennis Seckler.

the features are usually truncated—cut off at the top by subsequent building floors—they were used for trash by former residents, and in the trash are clues to everyday lives—what residents ate, what they valued, saved, and what they threw out. The trash is our basic source of data, and interpreting it along with the primary and secondary historical sources can tell us a good deal about people's lives.

Preliminary research may suggest the presence of a brothel in a project area, but it is more often discordant and distinctive artifacts that lead to the identification of a brothel that is then confirmed, if one is lucky, in the archives. Prostitution in brothels like those we have been able to investigate was part of being urban in the industrialized world. Often located in neighborhoods characterized as slums, brothels were as universal as the slums themselves (Mayne 1993:1). Brothels are, of course, not the only resources present on urban sites, and urban sites are not the only ones affected by NHPA regulations. In addition to trash from a brothel dating to the 1830s found on the site of a new courthouse at Foley Square in Manhattan, for instance, there was evidence of an eighteenth-century bake oven, drinking paraphernalia from at least one nineteenth-century tavern, a large cesspool overflowing with thousands of artifacts associated with newly arrived Irish immigrants, and 12 more privy features full of trash from working-class households spanning the nineteenth century (Yamin, ed. 2000).

Projects done in compliance with NHPA have also produced evidence of a variety of other clandestine activities. At the Boott Cotton Mills, a National Park Service site in Lowell, Massachusetts, for instance, evidence was found of drinking in the boarding houses, which was strictly forbidden (Bond 1989), and alcohol bottles found at Harpers Ferry, another National Park Service site, suggested inappropriate drinking on the job (Shackel 2000). The evidence is not always artifactual and does not always involve major excavation. On a federally funded highway project in Delaware, maps and ground testing were used to identify a network of cart roads used for smuggling contraband goods across the state in the eighteenth century (Burrow et al. 2014). All of these projects, and many more, were initiated because of the NHPA, and all are discussed in greater detail in the following pages.

Although NHPA-sponsored archaeology counts for a good proportion of the archaeology done in the United States in the last thirty years or so, it is not the only archaeology. Changing research interests and changing political contexts have inspired archaeologists to investigate traditional sites from new perspectives. Plantation sites that were originally considered in the context of historic preservation and restoration became places to figure out how "the cultural, economic, and political milieu" of plantation societies operated (Singleton 1990:70). Archaeological evidence for clandestine activities was found in both slave quarters and "big" houses, especially on plantation sites in the southern United States, but also in the Northeast (Matthews and McGovern 2015). The close study of slave quarters, in particular, has brought to light all kinds of clandestine practices associated with resisting power and maintaining personal agency.

The interest in African American archaeology emerged as a major focus in the discipline in the 1990s and has continued to grow. This includes projects associated with the Underground Railroad, itself a clandestine activity. Archaeology is well positioned to distinguish mythical stops on the Underground Railroad from actual stops, and it has proved to be particularly powerful at exposing the involvement of African Americans as organizers, as well as escapees. The excavation of African burial grounds has also produced new information on African-related burial practices (for example, Blakey and Rankin-Hill 2009).

Another area that has produced evidence of clandestine activities is the intense study of a few small cities. Long-term studies in both Alexandria (Virginia) and Annapolis (Maryland) are good examples. In Annapolis, for instance, a generation of archaeologists under the guidance of Mark Leone at the University of Maryland have investigated many private properties, including historic houses and their yards (2005). These studies, which the archaeologists have used to examine how we think about the past and interpret it in the present, have uncovered caches of artifacts relating to spiritual activities as well as domestic practices.

Changes in technology have also opened up parts of the past that were previously inaccessible. While it would have been possible to find evidence of piracy and smuggling on terrestrial sites if we knew what goods to look for, underwater archaeologists have used increasingly sophisticated techniques to find and analyze shipwrecks with exactitude that was unimaginable not very long ago (for example, Ewen 2006). The goods recovered from pirate ships reveal a different picture of life than is portrayed in popular accounts and goes well beyond descriptions of the booty on board.

All of these clandestine activities involve agency, but we all have agency in spite of constraining circumstances of one sort or another. What sets apart the people discussed here is their willingness to depart from society's norms. Prostitution was not necessarily illegal or hidden, but it was still not a respectable way of making a living, at least in the eyes of the public. Defying work rules in either civilian or military situations was not necessarily illegal either, but it was risky, and there was always a chance of losing a job or being discharged. One scholar has argued that agency in the past is what makes us able to live with ourselves in the present (Moore 2000:261). Perhaps, but for us—for anthropologists—it may be that we can't help but admire the creative capacity of humans no matter where they are in time or place.

Agency and Individual Action

Archaeologists have always excavated the remains of individual behavior, but the focus of analysis has changed over time. In the 1960s and 1970s, prehistoric archaeologists, in particular, attempted to use scientific methodology, including the testing of hypotheses about human behavior, to find causal explanations for events in the past (Hodder 1999; McGuire 1992). They were interested in such things as adaptive systems, cultural regularities on a large scale, and generalized pattern analysis. To an extent, historical archaeologists followed suit, at least in terms of methodology, but the problem with the approach was that it failed to allow for human agency, for what Matthew Johnson calls "the direct and indirect results of countless individual actions—the choice whether to zig or zag on ceramic decoration, the angle of retouch on a flint blade, the decision to dig a pit here rather than there" (Johnson 2007:241). Leaving out agency is leaving out what is perhaps most exciting about doing archaeology, that is, using material remains to connect with individual people in the past and figure out what their lives were like.

Attention to agency and individual action in archaeology emerged in the 1980s, a period when a general movement in Western culture referred to as postmodernism called for the replacement of grand theories about the state of culture and humanity with wider attention to the meaning of individual actions. Postmodernism recognizes the contributions of individuals and diverse cultures to a heterogeneous world (Storey 1998:346). The approach was called post-processualism in archaeology, a term coined by British archaeologist Ian Hodder to cover a practice he described as "interpretive and self-reflective," with emphasis being placed on the individual, agency, historical contexts, and meaning (Hodder 1999:5). The concept of agency, in the sense of conforming and not conforming to convention, is central to post-processual practice.

While unconventional acts are possible, they are not usual. As stressed by Anthony Giddens and Pierre Bourdieu, the two sociologists most often credited with the development of a theory of agency, humans do not act as free agents. They act instead within social structures inherited from the past (McGuire 1992:133). Giddens' theory of structuration stresses that individuals are heavily constrained by existing mental and material structures (Johnson 2007:245). They are influenced by these structures and at the same time have the power to "produce and reproduce them" (Gardner 2007:34). Agency is both conscious and unconscious, with individual actions producing both intentional and unintentional consequences. Agency is thus possible, but only within culturally defined constraints, what we generally refer to in archaeology as "historical contexts" (Hodder 1999:5).

Bourdieu talks less about social structure and more about "habitus," a concept that emphasizes the unconscious aspect of agency. Habitus is defined as the "taken-for-granted routines of daily life," the system of dispositions that guide thought and action (Dobres and Robb 2000:5). For Bourdieu, there is agency, but it is "expressed (and reproduced) through embodied and routinized social practices" (Jordan 2007:114). This is a particularly useful concept for historical archaeology, because the material record we excavate, the one that survives in the ground, often consists of consumer goods—sets of dishes, for instance—from which we speculate about how people organized their everyday lives, how they conformed to society's expectations or departed from them. Bourdieu provides a mechanism for describing individual actions within social frameworks inherited from the past while modifying those social frameworks or giving them new meaning in the process.

Finding evidence of nonconformity to prescribed ways of doing things, thinking, buying, etc., is admittedly a relief from the conformity that many historical archaeological studies reveal, but as we will demonstrate through the many examples in this book, evidence of agency is present where it wouldn't even seem possible. To derive meaning from the evidence is the challenge, and, as has often been said, the artifacts do not speak for themselves. We have to interpret what they mean.

Meaning is dependent on cultural context and probably also dependent on who is doing the interpreting. Actors with agency conform, but they also innovate, resist, and interpret social situations differently, all within specific cultural contexts. Cultural contexts are complicated and may involve several factors interacting with one another. Gender, the "cultural interpretation of perceived biological differences," for instance, does not operate alone but intersects with class, ethnicity, and race, at the very least, and also with other factors, like age, identity, and life cycle (Rotman 2015:2). Gender, class, and race are therefore not really separate categories, as demonstrated by the examples below.

Gender

In historical archaeology, the "cult of domesticity," a concept prescribing the appropriate behavior of women in the nineteenth century, has provided a context in which to examine the agency of middle-class women. Adherence to the cult of domesticity required women to confine themselves to the private (home) sphere, leaving the public sphere to men. Women's responsibility was mainly to create a peaceful haven for their men, who toiled in the competitive capitalist world, and to raise their children in a pious environment that would instill in them proper values, manners, and appropriate gender behavior (Spencer-Wood 1991:237; Wall 1991, 1994). Since the choice of household goods and their subsequent appearance in artifact assemblages might reveal conformance or nonconformance to the ideal, the cult of domesticity has proved useful to archaeological analysis. Dishes in gothic-style designs, for instance, are interpreted as relating to the creation of a pious household; and dolls and marbles, to teaching boys and girls how to behave differently from each other.

While it would be possible to just describe artifacts as either fitting or not fitting the ideal model, Diana diZerega Wall's study of gender (1991) uses Bourdieu's concept of "distinction" to show how women from the lower and upper ends of the middle-class spectrum used tablewares and teawares to create and maintain their different class positions in mid-nineteenth-century New York City. The study also shows how gender is intertwined with class and includes men as well as women (Mrozowski et al. 2000:xix; Wall 1994). Both the lower- and upper-middle-class households in Wall's study owned fashionable, everyday ironstone dishes for family meals, but the upper-middle-class household had a separate set of porcelain teaware for entertaining guests. Wall suggests that the woman in the upper-middle-class household was using her fancier teawares (and her agency) to impress her friends and acquaintances with her family's gentility (Wall 1991:79). In that way she aided her husband's reputation and expressed her own superior position in the class system.

Deborah Rotman's (2015) book on the archaeology of gender in this series shows how gender structures social life and access to economic resources on many different levels: the household, the community, public institutions. Her study reveals the agency of women at these different scales, which she illuminates through a variety of examples. Female domestic reformers, for instance, brought their moral values into the community by promoting the creation of public parks and playgrounds as places to bring people "into contact with the purifying influence of God's nature" (Rotman 2015:83, quoting Suzanne Spencer-Wood).

Class

The concept of class is central to historical archaeology, which takes as its ultimate purpose the study of "the material dimensions of capitalism" and how it works and endures in the modern world (Mrozowski et al. 2000:xiv). One's position in a culturally defined social and economic hierarchy puts limits on what one can do and buy. In this context, people's personal possessions become active expressions of where they fit in the class hierarchy. What is particularly valuable about a historical archaeological study of class is that it has the potential to treat class just as E. P. Thompson, the author of *The Making of the English Working Class* (1963), would have us treat it: not as an abstraction, but as a dimension of the real-life experience of people (McGuire 1992:44).

Paul Shackel's (2000) study of ceramic use among wage workers at the manufacturing town of Harpers Ferry is a good example of how workers at the bottom of the class hierarchy used their agency to reject the ideology of mass production and mass consumption. The workers at Harpers Ferry operated in a rigid class structure, with conflict often arising between workers (craftsmen, pieceworkers, wage laborers) and managers (Shackel 2000:232). Uncomfortable working conditions and a seven-day workweek (14 to 18 hours Monday through Saturday, and 6 hours on Sunday) gave workers plenty to complain about. Shackel's comparative study of ceramics associated with pieceworker and wage-worker households shows subtle differences before and after 1841, when a new wage-labor system was introduced.

The pieceworker households had relatively fashionable dishes before 1841, and the wage workers had very similar ones after 1841, when they would have been considered unfashionable. Although the wage workers could have afforded more-fashionable dishes, Shackel suggests that the women in the wage-worker households who purchased them chose not to subscribe to the consumer culture that had become synonymous with the new industrial order. Consistent with Bourdieu's concept of habitus, they were active agents in making choices to suit their everyday lives (Shackel 2000:242). Whether they consciously or unconsciously made these choices cannot be known, but applying the idea of agency to the observed differences in the assemblages used by different members of the Harpers Ferry workforce allowed Shackel to explain differences that might have been interpreted in another way.

Race

Race may be the most powerful context for the study of agency. As a cultural construct, it has had a profound influence on American historical archaeology, from the study of enslaved Africans on southern plantations to the study of racialized immigrant populations in urban slums. The following example shows how the custom of yard sweeping, often attributed to west African roots, may be given more complicated meaning by using Bourdieu's concept of "improvisation." The example is drawn from Christopher Barton and David Orr's work at Timbuctoo, an African American community in southern New Jersey (2015).

Yard sweeping, Barton and Orr argue, is more than a practice inherited from West Africa (2015:198). Swept yards adjacent to African American houses, recovered archaeologically as cleanly swept artifact- and plant-free spaces, may have originally related to west African spiritualism, but they were also dynamic spaces used for all sorts of work-related and social activities (Barton and Orr 2015:203, citing Battle-Baptiste 2010, 2011). In Timbuctoo, a nineteenth-century community of formerly enslaved Africans, Barton and Orr suggest a swept yard could counter the middle-class ideal of a well-groomed lawn. Swept yards for the economically marginalized were extensions of family homes. One of the authors (Orr) of the Timbuctoo study describes swept yards as places to play, places to get out of the heat of a small house (Barton and Orr 2015:208). They were functional necessities rather than ideological statements for people who couldn't afford spacious houses or tree-shaded yards (Barton and Orr 2015:206). What links various examples of yard sweeping is a state of social and economic marginalization.

Citing Bourdieu's practice theory of improvisation, which refers to the practice of "making do" in situations of marginalization, Barton and Orr conclude that yard sweeping is an example of "a tradition of life on the economic periphery" and that yard sweeping at Timbuctoo had more to do with economic marginality than African tradition (2015:210). Race in this case is less important than class, but they are inextricably intertwined.

Agency in the Extreme

The studies by Wall, Shackel, and Barton and Orr discussed above are examples of using agency theory to tease out meaning from the archaeological remains. Agency is revealed in everyday activities—serving tea, choosing dishes, sweeping yards. Much of the evidence of agency discussed in this book, however, is not subtle. It is a kind of agency in the extreme. Prostitutes in nineteenth-century New York knew about the cult of domesticity; they acted like ladies, dressed fashionably, and bought their children didactic toys. However, they definitely did not confine themselves to the sanctuary of a private home. Besides eating on unfashionable dishes, wage workers at Harpers Ferry rebelled against industrial ideology by drinking on the job and hiding the evidence between the walls of their work spaces while at the same time doing their jobs.

The concept of agency is used here to tie together the various case studies, but the concept, for the most part, did not guide the studies we cite. Even scholars are influenced by changes in fashion, and studies are often done using whatever theory is fashionable at the time or, in some cases, using no explicit theory at all. The archaeological projects cited here were done by different people at different times using different theoretical approaches (for example, practice, Marxist, discourse, interpretive, critical). What they have in common is a commitment to quantitative methods, exacting excavation techniques, and rigorous contextual analysis in the service of interpretation.

Why a Book about the Unconventional?

The idea for this book began with prostitution, not because it is a racy subject, but because archaeology done in compliance with NHPA has taken us to places we could not afford to go before and has produced large artifact assemblages associated with brothels. The discovery of brothels and the subsequent analysis of materials recovered from them coincided with the post-processual emphasis being placed on the study of individual households in historical archaeology. Rather than using urban sites to characterize whole neighborhoods and/or anonymous groups of people, historical archaeologists turned their efforts in the 1990s to talking about specific people—to bringing the uncelebrated and unknown to life (Beaudry et al. 1991; Rotman 2009; Wall 1994). The approach was influenced by social historians, who a decade before had invented a new kind of history, a history that was not just an investigation of the politically (and usually white) powerful men and their elite families. Instead, it focused on the middle and working classes, on the demographics of society, and on the agency in the everyday lives of everyday people. Historical archaeologists, especially urban archaeologists, had the material to do the same. We too could mine census records and directories for the names and occupations of residents whose properties we were excavating, and we could use the material remains recovered to construct a picture of daily life.

Urban archaeology, however, is not the only archaeology that has produced information on daily lives or on unconventional behavior. Historical archaeologists have always used material evidence to get inside people's lives and learn things that are not in the documentary record. With and without NHPA, evidence of clandestine activities has been found in all sorts of unlikely places—under kitchen floors, behind walls, inside prison cells, and scratched in windowpanes, to name just a few. This book brings together these examples of unconventional behavior, rarely discussed out of context, to focus on the human capacity for agency in a variety of circumstances.

One of the major achievements of historical archaeology is the recognition of the capacity of the subaltern—people without conventional kinds of social and economic power—to control their own lives, to express themselves, and to defy the constraints upon them. While not all of the examples of clandestine behavior presented here are the work of the subaltern, many are. Many demonstrate how enslaved Africans expressed themselves in ways that were specific to their culture and, in some cases, escaped from slavery at great risk; how workers resisted oppressive work conditions and sabotaged their bosses in secret ways; and how women with few alternatives turned to selling sex to support themselves and their children.

We do not think that subaltern men and women, or any men and women for that matter, are "completely free to choose" how they live their lives (Orser 1996:168–173), but we do think that people—all people—have a certain amount of agency, some of which they use in secret ways. The next two chapters (chapters 2 and 3) look at the archaeological evidence for prostitution in parlor houses and brothels in the eastern United States. A pattern of front-stage/ backstage behavior has emerged from our own work in Washington, DC, and New York that has also been noted by archaeologists working on brothels in other cities, and we discuss that pattern in detail. Prostitution on the American frontier is discussed in chapter 4. Archaeological evidence suggests that prostitution in the saloons and brothels of the frontier West was different than in the East. It may have been more publicly acceptable, at least in some places and at some times, and prostitutes' lives may have been less conflicted. Chapter 5 deals with the age-old American tradition of public defiance of the rules, and chapter 6, with private practices that make life endurable.

The book ends with a consideration of acts of agency in the present, with particular attention to ongoing arguments for and against the legalization of prostitution. We also reflect on passing moral judgment on people's actions, an issue that has troubled anthropologists as long as they have been studying other cultures. We are students of the past, but we are well aware that the past is never just the past: it is the past viewed through our own presentist perspective. Since so much of what is discussed here was against the rules, there is the risk of being judgmental, but there is an even greater risk of romanticizing, both of which we try to avoid.

2

The Archaeology of Prostitution in American Cities

The excavation of brothel sites in the United States began with large urban projects. The interpretation of artifacts associated with prostitution was new to archaeology, but the historical study of prostitution was not new, and several sources proved invaluable for building social contexts for understanding the large artifact assemblages that were recovered from brothel sites. Among them was a book published by Dr. William Sanger in the middle of the nineteenth century, and a much more recent book by historian Christine Stansell, published in 1987. As historical archaeologists became more interested in the intimate details of brothel life, they turned to new sources for context, and those are also considered here. All of these ideas provide an introduction to describing the excavated finds from brothels in New York City; Washington, DC; St. Paul; Boston; and Los Angeles.

From William Sanger to Christine Stansell: A Social Perspective on Prostitution

William Sanger's study of prostitution, published in 1858, is the basic reference for the study of prostitution in nineteenth-century America, for both archaeologists and historians. Sanger's introductory chapters cover the world—including Egypt, Syria, Asia Minor, Greece, Rome, France, Spain, Portugal, Algeria, and Belgium—but the particular value of the study is the research he conducted among prostitutes confined to the hospital on Blackwell's Island in New York City (Figure 2.1). As New Yorkers confronted the effects of explosive population growth and overcrowding in the early decades of the nineteenth century, they built institutions to deal with the problems, including a penitentiary and hospital (1832) on Blackwell's Island. Dr. William Sanger

Figure 2.1. Penitentiary and hospital on Blackwell's Island, where William Sanger did his study. From J. F. Ptak Science Books LLC, Post 886, History of Holes, Part 8. Accessed online; in the public domain.

was appointed chief resident physician of the hospital in 1853 and was charged with determining why syphilis was rampant on the island. The question put to him was, "What are your views in reference to the best means of checking and decreasing this disease, and what plan, in your opinion, could be adopted to relieve New York City of the enormous amount of misery and expense caused by syphilis?" (Sanger 1939:28). Implied in the question was the assumption that prostitution was the cause. Sanger did not think there was an easy answer. In his words, "Unlike the vice of a few years since, it no longer confines itself to secrecy and darkness but boldly strides through our most thronged and elegant thoroughfares, and there in the broad light of sun it jostles the pure, the virtuous, and the good" (Sanger 1939:29).

While Sanger characterized prostitution as an evil, he did not claim to understand it. It was his duty, he said, to know the facts, and he asked the president of the hospital's board to involve the city's mayor in the taking of a census of the city's prostitutes. The resulting research was in every way remarkable. Sanger prepared a schedule of questions to be administered by the city's police force, which was then under the direction of a Captain Matsell. Both Sanger and Matsell were morally outraged by the existence of prostitution, but they were also determined to "present all possible information on the matter, and give a truthful, unexaggerated picture of the depravity" (Sanger 1939:32). The word "depravity" betrays them, but the questions themselves provided interviewees plenty of room to explain themselves. Two thousand questionnaires were administered, about 40% of them to prostitutes who had worked in New York City. The questions ranged from the expected demographic ones—age, place of birth, time in the United States, marital status, number of children—to more enlightening ones: Were your children born in wedlock? How long were you a prostitute? What was the cause of your becoming a prostitute? What were your average weekly earnings? Did you contract any disease incident to being a prostitute? What business did your father follow? Did your mother have any business independent of your father? Were your parents Protestants, Catholics, or non-professors? Were you trained in any religion?

The answers are fascinating and, in some cases, surprising. Almost as many prostitutes (513) cited "inclination" as the reason for choosing the profession as cited "destitution" (525). Another 258 said they had been seduced and abandoned; 181 had the desire to drink; 164 had been ill treated by their parents; and 124 saw it as "an easy life." While they may not have been telling the whole truth, they did not express shame. Sanger had a hard time accepting inclination as a true reason. Along with other members of the middle class, he believed that women did not feel desire, that it "exists only in a slumbering state until aroused by some outside influences" (1939:488), and that without those influences, "the full force of sexual desire is seldom known to a virtuous woman" (1939:489). It is an obvious example of the scientist not wanting to learn what he does not want to believe. It also shows that Sanger did not assume that prostitutes were evil people. He saw them as victims driven by destitution, the reason he found easiest to accept.

Archaeologists, too, seem to be more comfortable interpreting prostitution as a product of poverty than they are dealing with the complexity of the practice. We have used Sanger more for his information about the physical places prostitutes worked—various levels of brothels—than who they actually were. It is easier to fit our artifacts with places than to interpret the people. The most luxurious brothels, according to Sanger, were parlor houses. They "were furnished with a lavish display of luxury but not good taste." The prostitutes—three-quarters of them natives of the United States—paid $10 to $16 to live there, worked from noon to midnight or later, drank champagne with their clients, wore fashionable clothes, and were served a "neat and well-arranged breakfast about 11 or 12 o'clock and dinner at 5 or 6 by an experienced staff of servants, usually colored" (Sanger 1939:554). Sanger's assumptions about the residents again reveal his middle-class values. "When they have no visitors," he wrote, "they generally indulge in a luxurious indolence. For any useful employment, such as sewing or fancy needlework, they have but little inclination, and their general refuge from ennui is formed in reading novels" (Sanger 1939:552). In spite of the fashionable clothes and other luxuries, Sanger was sure the women were deeply unhappy, as they knew their male admirers regarded them as but "a purchased instrument to minister to his [their] gratification" (Sanger 1939:553).

A second class of house attempted the same standard as the first but was "not as lavish." The prostitutes "whose charms had begun to fade" drank wine or brandy with their clients instead of champagne and put up with less experienced servants (Sanger 1939:553). Its occupants were presumably equally indolent, albeit less well dressed.

Brothels in the third class were located in less fashionable neighborhoods. Except for the location, Sanger thought these houses were equal and sometimes superior to the second class. The prostitutes were young and foreign born, the largest proportion being Irish and German, and they may even have occupied themselves productively when not working. He claims to have seen two or three girls in different parts of the reception room for a German brothel "knitting or sewing." Below the third-class houses were a variety of unsavory establishments, as well as street walkers, who rented individual rooms, and women who entertained in the third tier of theaters (Sanger 1939:560).

Sanger was a scientist confused by the values of his class. Nevertheless, his classification of the different types of brothels has been useful to archaeologists. His portrayal of prostitutes as victims, though sympathetic, has been less useful in an age when archaeologists, and especially feminist archaeologists, are looking for evidence of agency. Although the interviews revealed plenty of agency among women who made their livings as prostitutes, Sanger and other social thinkers of the day refused to accept what the women were saying as true. Some archaeologists have also been unwilling to shake off the presumption that nineteenth-century prostitutes were pathetic, impoverished, and morally bankrupt. That opinion is not shared, however, by historian Christine Stansell, whose book *City of Women: Sex and Class in New York, 1789–1860* (1987) focuses on laboring women, including prostitutes among them.

Stansell is a social historian whose book was inspired by the dearth of working women in scholarship about the nineteenth century. When they do appear, she says, "it is usually as timid and downtrodden souls, too miserable and oppressed to take much part in making history" (Stansell 1987:xii). Stansell thinks that laboring women's public presence was actually one of the things that set people against the poor. From the outside, life in the tenements looked raucous and loud. While bourgeois women in the early decades of the nineteenth century were creating private sanctuaries—the genteel home—in which to exert newfound power over the family's moral and social being, laboring women were depending on each other. Without the luxury of privacy, women in the tenements lived much of their lives in public: they knew everybody else's business, and everybody else knew theirs (Figure 2.2). They held families together, not with a set of rules for good table manners and appropriate feminine and masculine behavior, but with resourcefulness and interdependency. They sent children on errands, encouraged them to scavenge whatever they could, and survived day to day by pawning possessions

Figure 2.2. *Harper's Weekly* image of Rag Picker's Court, Mulberry Street, New York, 1879. From *New York in the Nineteenth Century*, by John Grafton 1977:63. Dover Publications, New York.

early in the week and retrieving them at week's end. Most important of all, women shared and loaned to neighbors. They moved around the tenements, gossiped, drank, and kept each other company; there were no secrets (Stansell 1987:57). They also sometimes came to blows, taking their fights to the street where neighbors could observe both sides of an argument and protect their own kind (Stansell 1987:58).

This perspective on the reality of women's lives puts the choice of prostitution in a different light. Working-class women needed husbands' incomes, but when they no longer had them—due to a man's loss of job, injury, or abandonment—they did what they could to support their families. They were not ashamed of their condition; on the contrary, they were energized, but it was hard. Some women wanted to get out from under the obligations of a struggling family. They wanted to live apart from their families and took low-paying jobs to do so. They worked in textile shops sewing shirts for as little as six cents apiece (Stansell 1987:111) and in factories as straw sewers for a slightly higher wage. The income, no matter how paltry, gave these women a sense of independence and the nerve to be "venturesome." The factory girl was "impudent rather than timid, sociable rather than retiring." She was a threat to a society that revered separate sexual spheres with women confined to the domestic one (Stansell 1987:128). Working girls, and even wives, turned to prostitution to make extra money, and some women turned to it full-time. It was generally assumed that most working-class women had been prostitutes at one time or another.

This more sympathetic portrait of working-class hardships has provided archaeologists with a kind of objective context in which to put the material evidence of prostitution. It was done out of necessity, not out of moral depravity; it was a fact of life and was hardly less respectable than sewing shirts or keeping boarders. It certainly made more money and may even have been less taxing. The emphasis was not on the sex itself, but on what it could buy and how desirable those things—especially clothes—were to impoverished young women who were otherwise entangled in family obligations. The words of women who spoke to this issue are included at the end of chapter 4 and in the discussion below.

Closer to an insider's perspective is a book published by anthropologist Oscar Lewis in 1965. *La Vida*, a study of the Rios family, grew out of Lewis's larger study of 100 Puerto Rican families who moved back and forth between four working-class neighborhoods (he calls them slums) in Greater San Juan and

New York. Three of the Rios women, Fernanda and her daughters, Felicita and Soledad, worked as prostitutes at some time in their lives. The interviews with them touch on their reasons for turning to prostitution, the practice itself, and how it affected each one's sense of self-respect. Much of the book is in the words of the interviewees. Each tells her (and in at least one case, his) own story.

At the time she was interviewed, Fernanda was living with her sixth husband, twenty-one years her junior, in a neighborhood called La Esmeralda. She talks exuberantly about their sex lives, about their living situation, and about the neighborhood. There was no privacy, and continual noise and occasional violence in the street, but there was also gaiety and lots of camaraderie. Family members were constantly moving in and out, everyone overheard everyone else's business, and everyone seems to have had very complicated love lives. Fernanda does not complain about her years as a prostitute. She did it for the money—to buy her children presents for Christmas—and like other women in the neighborhood, she did it only some of the time. The sex, she says, was not like sex at all. "A whore," Fernanda claims, "really doesn't feel pleasure except when she feels the money in her hands. It's like not having a sex life at all" (Lewis 1965:55).

Like their mother, Fernanda's daughters turned to prostitution to support their children. Felicita, the youngest, had five children by the time she was 22 and, at her mother's urging, became a prostitute to support them. Advising her daughter, Fernanda said, "All you have to do is get ready, put the children to bed, and wait until they fall asleep. Then you lock them in with a padlock. You can go out hustling every night" (Lewis 1965:351). Felicita, and also her sister, Soledad, were not ashamed of being prostitutes as much as they were embarrassed by having to take off their clothes in front of strangers. They did admit, however, that the neighbors wouldn't have anything to do with a woman if they knew she was "in the profession" (Lewis 1965:356). True or not, Lewis found that 33% of the families in his sample had a history of prostitution.

Stansell (who does not cite Oscar Lewis) and even Sanger would recognize the Rios women. They are spirited, resourceful, and anything but pathetic. They are also passionate, about their children and about the men they love, but not about their clients. For them, sex for money is not the same as sex for love, and one does not seem to interfere with the other. This intimate perspective on the life of prostitutes is not a perspective that either social historians (with some notable exceptions) or archaeologists have allowed themselves.

Social historians and their archaeologist followers take a feminist perspective—attention to women's work, respect for women's choices, appreciation for economic realities, a kind of nonjudgmental amoral attitude—but it is not the same as a perspective that pays more attention to the sex in prostitution and to performance as it alters a prostitute's sense of self or, more accurately, her sense of selves.

Gender is not the same in all societies, it is not always binary, and it is not always unchanging (Rotman 2015:2–8). Biology produces physical differences, but it does not determine how those differences are culturally interpreted. According to one scholar, gender is performative (Butler 1999). It is constituted through actions, through what Judith Butler calls the "gendered stylization of the body" (1999:xv). Like Bourdieu's concept of "habitus," gender happens through habitual repetitions of behavior. It may be that for prostitutes like the Rios women, more than one gender was possible. Repeated behaviors in the practice of prostitution constituted one way they were "women," and repeated behaviors in their everyday lives outside that work were another way. There is agency in the performative generation of gendered behavior and the many possibilities it opens up (Butler 1999:187).

The Sex and Performance in Prostitution

The recovery and identification of artifacts relating to sex and feminine hygiene have led archaeologists to confront the sex in prostitution. They have done it as scientists—with objective descriptions of the paraphernalia and how it related to the physical reality, including the dangers, of commercial sex. There is an opportunity, however, to breathe the life back into these artifacts and figure out how they fit into women's lives as actually lived. Lynn Meskell has demonstrated how sexuality permeated New Kingdom Egyptian experience to the extent "that it would have been unthinkable to isolate it" (Meskell 2000:255). She thinks we have misread Egyptian sexuality and cast it in our own experience. It is possible that we have done the same with the history of sex in our own society, and there may be a way to use archaeology to do better.

Some scholars have noted that sex has been avoided by archaeologists for a number of reasons, among them the idea that it is a dangerous subject (Schmidt and Voss 2000:3). They have pointed out that the archaeological literature on prostitution has provided "a window into the economics, social relations, and gendered politics of commercial sex" (2000:18); however, with one conspicuous exception, it hasn't done much to humanize the practice. The exception is Julia Costello's "play," which uses several first-person accounts and E. J. Bellocq's picture book about brothels in New Orleans's celebrated Storyville neighborhood to create a backdrop for a discussion of artifacts recovered from a six-seater privy in Los Angeles (Costello 2000). Costello's artifacts included quantities and varieties of beauty creams, cures for venereal disease, and pain-numbing tinctures of opium and morphine (Figure 2.3).

Historian Tim Gilfoyle's (1992) account of the rampant sexuality in the middle decades of the nineteenth century in New York City crosses some boundaries that haven't generally been crossed by archaeologists. He describes "model artist" shows in which "a lone actress assumed a stationary pose dressed in tights, transparent clothing, or nothing at all" (Gilfoyle 1992:127) and burlesque shows where as many as 100 scantily dressed women danced for an audience of ogling men. Even more extreme were brothel entertainments in which groups

Figure 2.3. Health and beauty items from a parlor house at 327 Aliso Street, Los Angeles, California. Courtesy of Mary Praetzellis, Anthropological Studies Center, Sonoma State University.

of women disrobed and touched each other erotically (Gilfoyle 1992:162). In concert saloons, which flourished in New York from the 1830s to the turn of the twentieth century, female performers and waitresses doubled as prostitutes (Gilfoyle 1992:225).

It was by no means just men who benefited from commercialized sex. Madams made money as proprietors of brothels, and all kinds of women attended the masquerade balls that were popular from the 1860s onward. According to contemporary observers, "through fantasies of dress, New Yorkers temporarily dropped their standard conceptions of proper 'respectable behavior,' . . . women wore black tights, red tights, and blue tights, men and women came in 'every picturesque garb imaginable'" (Gilfoyle 1992:272). The 1876 French Ball, which attracted 4,000 people, climaxed in a "bacchanalian orgy—a hot and crazy revel, a whirl of passion" (1992:232). For two decades (1866–1887), the French Balls were held at the Academy of Music, succeeded by the Metropolitan Opera House in the late 1880s, and Madison Square Garden in the 1890s. It is as if everyone of every status was celebrating what capitalism had wrought, and they were celebrating it together.

The archaeology of prostitution has placed commercialized sex solidly in the context of industrial capitalism, but except for Julia Costello's play, we have not used our finds to talk about what it was really like to be a prostitute, what its attractions were besides money. An essay by Priscilla Alexander in a book of essays by women in the sex industry (Delacoste and Alexander 1998) notes that

> programs to help people involved in prostitution fail to recognize its attractions—really good money and excitement. Preparing them to go into boring, low skill, low paying jobs will not succeed. Programs should be run by former sex workers who have experienced abuse, incarceration, stigmatization, isolation, etc., but programs should not just emphasize negatives because that denies prostitutes the agency involved and pride in who they have been. (Delacoste and Alexander 1998:223)

LuAnn DeCunzo's (1995) archaeological study of the Magdalen Society in Philadelphia draws similar conclusions. She found that the women who took shelter in the Magdalen Society, an institution meant to train "fallen women" for respectable womanhood, used their time there for their own purposes: as a respite from cold, hunger, and life in the streets (Rotman 2015:104, citing DeCunzo 1995:127). Most, if not all of them, returned to their old ways when it was convenient.

Prostitutes, according to a history of prostitution in Western society by former stripper and dancer Nickie Roberts (1992:338), do not necessarily lack self-respect, a point that came through in the Rios women's own words in *La Vida* and also in DeCunzo's study of the Magdalen Society. Progressive feminist scholarship, including that of women who have been prostitutes, is not afraid to emphasize the positive: "In spite of the fact that society does its utmost to make their work difficult and degrading, many whores feel positive about and proud of their work" (Roberts 1992:338). Interviews with prostitutes, conducted by Lewis Diana and reported by Nickie Roberts, found that 60% of the prostitutes he interviewed were "happy about their work, despite all the drawbacks" (Roberts 1992:338). Independence from men is a theme in much of the writing by prostitutes. They do it to have the finer things in life. "We're not brought into this life just so we can reproduce and cater to men. . . . We want to be independent, earn money and make a better life for ourselves and our children" (Califia 1994:327).

The evidence historical archaeologists have for nineteenth-century prostitution needs to be interpreted in the context of developing industrial capitalism and the concomitant commodification of sex, but it also needs to be seen from the inside as it is experienced, and the archaeological record provides the material to do that.

Prostitution Revealed through the Archaeology of Brothels

The excavation of brothel sites is the most direct way of examining the material culture of prostitution. A brothel may be defined as a household composed of boarding women who live together in their workplace. Their work is providing companionship and sexual services for male clients. Gender roles for women and men in the nineteenth century were generally understood to be complementary, with men employed outside the home in wage labor, and women employed at home in the unpaid labor of keeping house and raising children. This ideal was usually realized in middle- and upper-class households, but working-class households often needed more than the wages a man could earn. Women contributed to household income by doing laundry, taking in piecework, and keeping boarders. In households where men were absent, all members of the household, including children, needed to contribute. A working-class household without a male wage earner had a hard time paying for the basic necessities of life.

Unlike family households, brothel households were not made up of kin and were not responsible for the reproduction of society. Life in a high-class brothel was more comfortable than in a working-class household, especially one headed by a single adult woman. In a brothel, resident prostitutes ate regular meals and were able to dress well. In nineteenth-century cities, when young women attempted to live on their own and support themselves with factory or sales jobs, they found it hard to make ends meet. Working women did not make a living wage: they were paid half as much as men. Sometimes these women denied themselves clothing or food when cash ran short; sometimes, they allowed men to pay for leisure activities and even provide money for clothes in exchange for sexual favors (Seifert 1991:87). Some women turned to prostitution. A single female worker in the late nineteenth century made about $6 a week; as a resident in a brothel, she could make $40 to $50 a week or even more in some cities (Rosen 1982:147–148, 205, note 32).

Brothel Households in Comparative Context

In the 1980s and 1990s, archaeologists excavating sites in urban contexts in the East noted stark differences in material culture among urban households within a single neighborhood. Research in primary and secondary sources for projects in Washington, DC, for instance, documented high standards of living associated with brothels even when they were located in working-class neighborhoods. To understand the material correlates of working-class households and brothels, the archaeologists used the analytical methods for comparisons common at the time (e.g., Seifert 1991:97; Seifert and Balicki 2005:63–69). Pattern analysis, as originally defined by Stanley South (1977), with an emphasis on consumer choice (Spencer-Wood 1987), was standard practice, especially for urban archaeologists who were dealing with huge assemblages of artifacts.

Pattern analysis organizes artifact assemblages into functional groups, and the early studies of brothel households presented the data in South's functional categories: architecture, kitchen, clothing, furniture, personal, arms, tobacco, and activities (e.g., Seifert 1991). South's categories have been criticized for making some artifacts, especially ones associated with women's work, invisible (Yentsch and Beaudry 2000), but these categories proved useful for identifying gross distinctions within and between assemblages. The functional categories allowed the archaeologists to compare brothel assemblages with each other and with assemblages from contemporaneous working and/ or middle-class households. The comparative valuation of ceramics, called economic scaling, also standard practice in the 1980s and 1990s (Miller 1980, 1991), was useful for comparing the costs of brothel ceramic assemblages with those from working- and middle-class households. The method calculates an index value for a ceramic assemblage by comparing the prices of the ceramics in the assemblage with the prices of the cheapest vessels that would have been available.

Using these methods, Seifert and her colleagues compared an artifact assemblage excavated from a brothel in Hooker's Division, a brothel district in Washington, DC, of the late nineteenth to early twentieth century, with several contemporary working-class assemblages, two from the same site and one from a white working-class neighborhood, and two from African American neighborhoods that had been excavated elsewhere in the city (Seifert 1991). This was one of the first studies of a brothel assemblage in the United States. The artifacts from the Hooker's Division brothel (1890s–1914) did not include particularly expensive tablewares and teawares, but there was evidence in the food remains to suggest that the brothel spent more on meals than was spent on meals in nearby working-class households. Also different from the working-class assemblages were the relatively large numbers of artifacts relating to clothing (mainly buttons made out of porcelain, shell, bone, hard rubber, and metal), personal artifacts including jewelry, religious articles, hair combs, parts of a syringe, cosmetic bottles, and pharmaceutical bottles that once held potions known to treat "social diseases," tobacco pipes, and lots of lighting glass suggesting night work (Seifert 1991:97–103).

An earlier assemblage from another Washington brothel investigated by Seifert and her colleagues belonged to a well-known and well-to-do madam named Mary Ann Hall (Seifert and Balicki 2005). Hall ran what Sanger would have classified as a high-class parlor house in the middle decades of the nineteenth century. The artifacts recovered from the site included fashionable white ironstone tablewares and porcelain, considerably more expensive than the dishes in the contemporaneous assemblages from working-class households in the neighborhood. The food remains from this brothel also suggested that meals were more expensive and more varied than those served in working-class households, and there was evidence for the consumption of champagne (bottles, corks, and wire bales), which was completely absent from the working-class households and also from the Hooker's Division brothel (Seifert and Balicki 2005:71). The results of these Washington, DC, projects are discussed in greater detail in chapter 3.

The site of Nina Clifford's bordello was excavated on the proposed site of the Science Museum of Minnesota in St. Paul. Archaeologists analyzed artifacts recovered from excavations both in front of the brothel (the street side) and in the backyard (Ketz et al. 2005). The medicinal bottles, utilitarian ceramics, and food remains found behind the house seemed to relate to prostitutes' everyday private lives. The fancier ceramics (porcelain and refined earthenwares) and items associated with public display (including a vase, a flowerpot, and decorative figurine fragments) found in front of the house probably came from the public rooms in the brothel. The archaeologists concluded that the bad health conditions suggested by the medicinal bottles provide insights into the uncomfortable reality of resident prostitutes' lives behind the scenes. Nina Clifford's establishment may have had a reputation as a center of "the glamorous sporting life," but the brothel inmates' personal lives were considerably less glamorous (Ketz et al. 2005:87).

Internal differences were also found in the assemblage from the brothel found on the Moynihan Courthouse site in Lower Manhattan (Yamin 2005). Although the site was once part of the infamous Five Points neighborhood, portrayed in the yellow journalism of the day as New York City's worst slum, no brothels had been previously recorded on the project block. Like the Washington projects, the area excavated included more than one historic property, thus enabling comparisons among them. In this case, however, comparisons were made even before the artifacts had been quantified. The laboratory space supplied by the General Services Administration in the second basement of the U.S. Customs House at the World Trade Center made it possible to lay out the collections from more than one historic feature at a time. The ceramic artifacts from one of the features in particular were so different from the ceramics from every other feature in this working-class neighborhood that we suspected they came from a brothel (this project is discussed in detail in chapter 3). Among the unusual ceramics were an elegant Chinese porcelain tea-and-coffee set, many small transfer-printed plates that may have been used for snacks or as coasters for wine bottles, and 37 chamber pots. There were also lots of wine bottles (other households had more beer) and wide-mouthed flacons that probably held brandied fruits or other delicacies. A ceramic pot labeled, "AMAILLE s.d. Vinaigrier," presumably held a potion for douching, and there was at least one vaginal syringe in the assemblage, probably used for cleansing or contraception. Among the most telling artifacts were two glass urinals probably used by women confined to bed with venereal disease. The two complete skeletons of newborn infants recovered from the privy may have been the results of infanticide (Crist 2005).

Yamin's analysis of the assemblage produced a bimodal distribution of both ceramics and food remains, suggesting that the resident prostitutes were fed meals similar to those being eaten in nearby tenements when they were not working, and much fancier fare—veal, lobster, soft-shell crabs—when they were (2005:14). The tobacco pipes recovered also fell into two distinct groups, heavily charred ones that didn't have much decoration or tooth wear, and more decorative ones that were more worn. Yamin speculated that the plain ones belonged to the prostitutes, who may not have worn down mouthpieces in the way that has been noted for their male counterparts, while the decorative ones were left behind by clients. In addition to pipes, the presence of bird-watering devices, sewing implements (hooks, pins, a carved bone stiletto, a thimble, and a thread winder), a nursing shield, and children's china made it possible to envision the daily pastimes of the inmates as they waited for the working hours to begin (2005:15–16).

Excavations conducted at Union Station Los Angeles uncovered deposits including both cribs (single rooms with a door and window, outfitted with a bed, washstand, and chair) and a parlor-house brothel at 327 Aliso Street. Three backyard privies associated with the brothel produced 10,000 artifacts, which the analysis compared to artifacts from working-class households on adjacent lots (Meyer et al. 2005). Not surprisingly, the parlor house assemblage pointed to an emphasis on drinking, including decorative glass vessels and lots of wine bottles. The ceramics were more expensive than those associated with the working-class households also studied in this project, and the analysts suggested that they reflected a kind of "staged affluence" (Meyer et al. 2005:118). Unusual were nine quart-sized bottles that had contained Darby's Prophylactic Fluid, a multi-use disinfectant that was probably injected with the rubber syringes that were found. Also recovered were 12 Vaseline bottles, apparently used with boric acid to guard against both venereal disease and pregnancy (Figure 2.3).

Intimate Artifacts and Prostitution

Although comparing functional categories of artifacts found on nineteenth-century urban sites associated with brothel households to working- and middle-class households revealed differences, especially in categories of artifacts relating to eating and drinking, and internal differences in brothel assemblages that suggest "front-stage" and "backstage" behavior, the comparative approach did not tell us very much about the intimate lives of prostitutes. It is the close examination of artifacts often lumped together in different functional categories—such as kitchen, personal, activities—that provides insights into the care these working women took with cleanliness, contraception, venereal disease, lactation, and abortion. The presence of intimate artifacts is not what identifies a site as a brothel, but their analysis in a brothel context surely adds to an understanding of prostitution as it was experienced in nineteenth-century America.

At Boston University, Mary Beaudry used finds from a mid-nineteenth-century privy at 27/29 Endicott Street that had been excavated as part of the Central Artery project in Boston in the early 1990s to teach an undergraduate historic artifact analysis class. Because the Central Artery project was so huge, only artifacts dating before 1830 had been analyzed for the excavation report, leaving the rest of the material to be analyzed by others. Research into census data, tax records, and Boston directories indicated that a parlor-house brothel had operated on the property between 1853 and 1870. The brothel was first run by a woman named Mary A. Adams, then by Louisa Cowan, and finally by Mary Lake, a former prostitute who married the botanical druggist William Padelford in 1865 (Luiz 2016). The assemblage from the privy is generally associated with the Padelford period of occupancy.

The Padelford privy's contents were analyzed after the turn of the twenty-first century, when historical archaeologists were looking for ways to analyze artifact collections that did not rely on functional categories. Several students analyzed paraphernalia associated with what one of them characterizes as "a woman's intimate association with her own body and embodiment of self" (Luiz 2014). Perfume given by a client, for instance, even if originally chosen by the prostitute, removed her agency from the choice. Douching required by the brothel madam made the maintenance of the prostitute's own body someone else's decision; whether a prostitute was allowed to nurse her own baby might also be the madam's decision. Breast shields made out of glass found in the Padelford privy would have been worn by a prostitute when she was nursing a baby or when she was trying to suppress her milk. For either purpose, glass shields would have been uncomfortable and would have functioned to hide her identity as a mother (Luiz 2014).

Other artifacts associated with feminine personal care recovered from the Padelford privy were 30 glass syringes (Figure 2.4). The syringes ranged in

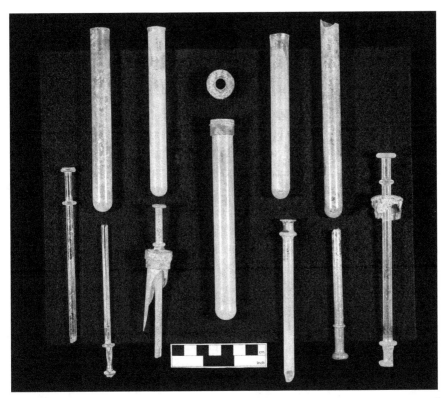

Figure 2.4. Syringes from the Padelford privy, Boston. Photo by Michael Hamilton. Courtesy of Mary C. Beaudry, Boston University.

length from 12.8 cm to 15.5 cm with diameters from 1.4 cm to 2 cm (Luiz 2014). The long tubes of mouth-blown glass had four or five perforations at the closed end and a threaded lead cap with a cork gasket at the open end. These were identified as vaginal syringes, which were introduced in the 1830s but were not widely used until the late nineteenth century (Eichner 2014).

Vaginal douching was used in the nineteenth century for a variety of purposes: cleansing with water, treating venereal disease, contraception, and inducing a miscarriage. Vaginal douching was not limited to prostitutes in the nineteenth century but was an established hygiene practice among middle- and upper-class women that was probably most often used for contraception (Geiger 2013:14, citing Brodie 1994). Other methods used for contraception included cacao butter solution, boric acid, olive oil, glycerin, tannic acid, carbolic acid, and bichloride of mercury (Eichner 2014).

Irrigating tonics used for venereal disease included mercury-based solutions and blood purgatives and purifiers, such as sarsaparilla and sassafras, used as a remedy for the mercury poisoning that was common after a mercury-based syphilis treatment (Geiger 2013:16). A still-corked apothecary bottle retrieved from the 27/29 Endicott Street privy contained Copaiba Oil, also known as Balsam, which was a pine-based resin and astringent known to have been used as treatment for venereal disease. A prostitute who had douched with this solution would undoubtedly have smelled of it. There were also ingestible cures for venereal disease, including mercury, arsenic, and sulfur, although none appears to have been recovered from the Padelford privy. There were, however, bottles for potions that were thought to induce abortions, among them Radway's Ready Relief and Madame Porter's Cough Balsam and Vegetable Pulmonary Balsam (Luiz 2014). The latter contained linseed oil, a common ingredient in homemade abortion recipes (Johnson 2010).

Artifact assemblages associated with brothel sites generally contain cosmetics and perfume. Six bottles containing expensive perfume were recovered; four of them were the large size from which the perfume was decanted into smaller bottles. One of the large ones, embossed "E. ROUSSEL/PHILAD," came from a shop in Philadelphia, and two other large bottles were marked "Lubin Parfumeur," presumably French.

Broadening the Context

Most of the archaeological studies of brothels and other places where sex was sold focus on the furnishings and equipage of the establishments or, as just discussed, on the intimate artifacts associated with sex. Some recent scholarship, however, has focused on the sale of sex in a broader context. Alexander Keim (2016) considered the Boston neighborhood around the brothel at 27/29 Endicott Street. Noting the tendency of the urban upper and middle classes to characterize nineteenth-century working-class neighborhoods as slums, he analyzed the presence of women, including prostitutes with "flash," as players in the urban landscape (Figure 2.5).

While proper (middle-class) women had been relegated to the domestic sphere by the middle of the nineteenth century, working-class women were conspicuous for their "consumption of clothing and objects of personal adornment; social behavior that eschewed chaperones for female companionship; and the embrace of leisure activity made possible by earned wages"

Figure 2.5. Image entitled, "Tempting to Ruin! How Gotham's Palaces of Sin Are Garrisoned Out of the Hovels—The Gaudy Spider Spreading Her Webs for the Flies Who Make Her Loathsome Trade Profitable." Originally from an 1882 issue of the *National Police Gazette*. Granger, New York City.

(Keim 2016). Keim proposes that specific artifacts recovered from the Padelford privy, including a gold ring, pins with gold plating and imitation stones, glass beads and fasteners in the style of jet jewelry, and items like molded mother-of-pearl buttons, would have contributed to a "fashionable appearance while remaining within the means of a working-class woman, . . . along with the clothing they would have adorned or been paired with, [they] were used to achieve a personal presentation designed to attract attention, emphasize the shape of the female figure, and conspicuously consume the money earned through work—sex or otherwise" (Keim 2016).

Beyond the construction of identity, Keim used pharmaceutical bottles and toothbrushes recovered from the Padelford privy to track the movements of the resident prostitutes through the city. Purchases were made mostly on the blocks immediately surrounding 27/29 Endicott Street, but there was also evidence for traveling beyond Boston's North End into other parts of the city. Keim's purpose was not just to see where the Endicott prostitutes went, but to illuminate the role of these women with "flash" in the social construction of the urban landscape. An analysis of wear on the shoes recovered from the privy—fancy sewn ones with turned soles and cloth uppers, and cheap durable leather ones known as brogans—suggested to him that the prostitutes did not just wear the fancy ones indoors for clients. Wear indicated that they were also worn outside as "part of the presentation of a fashionable identity" (Keim 2016). Furthermore, Keim argued that "the frequent presence of female sex workers in working-class urban neighborhoods, and their close association with other working women, meant that their presence outside of the brothel while not engaged in sex work would have been one of the contributing factors in the development of working-class space and identity" (Keim 2016).

Not every site that produces lots of perfume or other cosmetics, however, is a brothel. A study of ten rouge pots found on a site in New Orleans is a good example (Dawdy and Weybring 2008). When the rouge pots were first discovered on the Rising Sun Hotel site, it was assumed that they had belonged to prostitutes. Since the Rising Sun Hotel in the famous song refers to a house of prostitution, it seemed reasonable to conclude that the Rising Sun Hotel in 1820s New Orleans was also a house of prostitution (Dawdy and Weybring 2008:383). The Rising Sun Hotel site that was excavated, however, had been many things—a French colonial garden in the mid-1700s; a Spanish colonial residence that burned in 1794; a guesthouse or inn run by a widow from 1796 to 1809; an early nineteenth-century coffeehouse and hotel; a later (1821–1828) hotel that operated under the name Rising Sun; and a shirt factory and molasses plant during the late nineteenth century. The 10 French faience rouge pots came from destruction and demolition strata securely dated to an 1822 fire (Dawdy and Weybring 2008:374). The pots were found close together and were thought to have come from a dressing room or bedroom that collapsed during the fire. The question was whether the pots belonged to prostitutes or to someone else.

"Frenchness" cosmetics were associated with promiscuity in the middle of the nineteenth century (Dawdy and Weybring 2008:375). In fact, anything French (including the French Balls described by Gilfoyle in 1860s New York) was associated with sex and promiscuity (1992:232). However, the social phenomenon of the "dandy" was at its peak in America in the 1820s. Dandyism was both a fashion and a lifestyle, in which lower- and middle-class men "carefully manicured their skin, hair, dress, and manners in an effort to elevate their status" (Dawdy and Weybring 2008:385). The rouge pots could have belonged to men and may therefore represent men and masculinity rather than women and sexuality.

The Archaeology of Brothel Life

Several themes have emerged from the archaeological study of assemblages recovered from brothels. One is the manipulation of the material indications of class, and the second is the flexibility of gender roles for women in the nineteenth century. Not surprisingly, research styles and trends have changed over the years, and brothels have been treated to many different interpretive approaches. All of them have contributed to the understanding of an institution we didn't know much about before. What we have learned is history, of course, but it is intimate history, history from the inside out, as Henry Glassie (1988) would say. The early comparative studies revealed the material circumstances of living in a brothel, a special kind of household, and how they compared with the material circumstances of working-class households. The fancy dishes and expensive food suggested that working-class girls who turned to prostitution were at least rewarded with a comfortable place to live, good food, and the resources to dress well. Whether this made up for the degradation and real dangers of the profession, we cannot know, but if Keim is right, working-class girls and prostitutes may not have been distinguishable in the street. Prostitutes may even have set the style for women with "flash" and been indistinguishable from women who did not make their living as sex workers.

Comparative studies also revealed that class distinctions were manipulated inside brothel households. While there is evidence that the furnishings and household equipment, such as dishes and glassware, were in many cases comparable to the quality of things in middle-class or even upper-class homes and would have been provided by the madam or other manager of the brothel, they were probably accessible to prostitutes only when they were working. Artifact analysis indicates that there were two material standards inside brothels, one that suggested considerable expense and another that did not. Prostitutes may have shared exotic foods, sipped tea out of porcelain teacups, and drunk expensive wine with clients, but they probably ate pedestrian meals, much like the meals they would have eaten with their working-class families, when they were not with clients. They performed not only as sex partners but also as companions for the men who visited the brothel. They put on a show in a "theater" that was constructed by the management. Behind the scenes they were wage laborers and treated accordingly.

The evidence of the prostitutes' private lives inside the brothel is mixed. Some suggests daytime companionship with other women in the brothel—sewing, embroidering, chatting to pass the time—but the vast majority of the material evidence reflects the challenges that prostitutes faced because of the specific work required. There were the tasks of keeping clean, avoiding pregnancy, and treating venereal disease. The material evidence for these activities—for instance, vaginal syringes and various potions used in douching or taken orally; contraceptive devices; and portable urinals—are dramatic and distressing indications of just how difficult and dangerous sex work was. Working-class girls may have acquired the nice clothes and independence they craved, but the rewards were short-lived (depending on youth and beauty) and the dangers were real. While it is believed that some women escaped the life of a prostitute in the early decades of the nineteenth century and made respectable marriages, this was not as true later in the century (Roberts 1992:243). A high percentage of prostitutes contracted syphilis or gonorrhea, and many had children.

The archaeology of nineteenth-century prostitution presents a complicated picture. In one sense the artifacts look much like the artifacts from a respectable Victorian household—matching sets of dishes, fancy tewares, wine, and liquor bottles—but there are generally more of them. In addi-

Figure 2.6. Children's cups that encouraged good behavior and ownership. From the Five Points brothel privy (Feature AG).

tion, there are lots of artifacts relating to women's clothing, women's hygiene, and women's health, but these might also be found associated with a family household. There might even be children's cups with names or didactic sayings on them, and toys meant specifically for girls or boys (Figure 2.6). A Victorian brothel presented an image to the public it wanted to attract, and the prostitutes within conformed to the image, but their identities were more complex. The archaeology suggests inherent contradictions in brothel life, what may be its most distinctive trait.

3

Case Studies

A Brothel in New York City's Most Notorious Neighborhood and Parlor Houses within Sight of the White House

Large construction projects in New York City and Washington, DC, in the 1990s encountered the archaeological remains of brothels that, along with accompanying documentary research, were extensive enough to provide an intimate picture of life inside an institution that was omnipresent in nineteenth-century American cities. The New York City brothel investigated was located in the heart of Five Points, the city's most notorious neighborhood, famous worldwide as a down-and-out slum. The brothels investigated in Washington, DC, were within blocks of the White House and served the politicians, bureaucrats, and others who came to do business with the government in the capital city.

Make-Believe in the Middling Brothels at Five Points in New York City

While much ink has been spent on the horrors of commercial sex at Five Points and elsewhere in the city, the assemblage of artifacts recovered archaeologically from a brothel privy on the Moynihan Courthouse site at Foley Square is the first assemblage from a Five Points brothel to be studied in depth (Yamin, ed., 2000). The privy was one of 22 features analyzed from the site, which was located very close to Paradise Square, the center of the Five Points neighborhood (Figure 3.1). George Catlin's famous painting highlights all the evils that were supposedly prevalent at the Points—prostitutes hanging out of upstairs windows, fistfights in the streets, grog shops (often labeled "grocery") on every corner, racial mixing, public romancing, and at least one pig mixing with the masses.

Figure 3.1. *Five Points 1827*. Painting by George Catlin, reproduced as lithograph. McSpedon and Baker, Valentine 1855. Photography © New-York Historical Society.

Sex was a major industry at Five Points in the middle of the nineteenth century. At least, that is what the journalists and reformers of the day claimed. It was always mentioned in descriptions of the infamous neighborhood and was always blamed for the moral degradation that was believed to thrive in the broken-down shanties and tenements at the Points. Of the Old Brewery, an industrial building that had been converted into a kind of multifamily apartment complex, George Foster wrote,

> Every room in every story has its separate family or occupant, renting by the week or month and paying in advance. In this one room, the cooking, eating, and sleeping of the whole family, and their visitors are performed. Yes—and their visitors: for it is no unusual thing for a mother and her two or three daughters—all of course prostitutes—to receive their "men" at the same time and in the same room. (Foster 1990[1850]: 122)

Foster was a reporter for the *New York Tribune*, and his republished articles have much to do with Five Points' enduring reputation as a center of iniquity.

Another newspaperman, Herbert Asbury, writing in the 1920s, added to Foster's colorful accounts and went so far as to make up characters who could not have been real but are inseparable from the image of Five Points that endures. There was Mose, who was eight feet tall, had flaming ginger-colored hair, and hands as "large as the hams of a Virginia hog" (Asbury 1928:34). He could "lift a horse car off the tracks and carry it a few blocks on his shoulders" and blow a becalmed ship into the harbor with a puff of his two-foot-long cigar (Asbury 1928:36). There were gangs with colorful names like the Plug Uglies, Roach Guards, Shirt Tails, and Dead Rabbits, and a woman called Hell-Cat Mary, who "filed her front teeth to points" and "wore long artificial nails, constructed of brass" (Asbury 1928:30). Asbury, too, counted prostitution among the major evils at the Points. "Around the Points and Paradise Square," he wrote, "were 270 saloons, and several times that number of blind tigers, dance halls, houses of prostitution and green groceries which sold more wet goods than vegetables" (Asbury 1928:10).

Timothy Gilfoyle, a historian writing in the late twentieth century, claims that "sex was a readily accessible part of the underground economy. From 1830 to 1839, for example, twenty-seven of the forty-three blocks (63%) surrounding Paradise Square housed prostitutes on at least one occasion" (Gilfoyle 1992:39). In the 1820s Five Points contained the most brothels in the city. In the 1830s, 1840s, and 1850s, there continued to be concentrations of brothels in the blocks immediately adjacent to Paradise Square (Figure 3.2). Foster and Asbury were apparently not totally wrong about the prevalence of sex for sale at Five Points, but Gilfoyle's account puts it in the context of what else was going on in the city. His book *City of Eros* (1992) is about prostitution and the commercialization of sex in the whole city of New York in the nineteenth century, not just in its most infamous poor neighborhood.

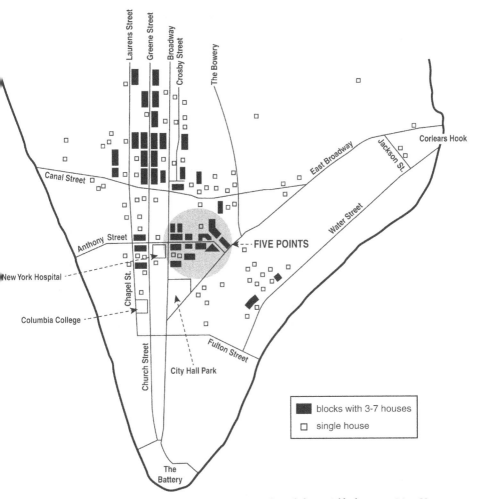

Figure 3.2. Map of houses of prostitution, 1850–1859. Adapted from Gilfoyle, 1992, Map V, 33. Redrawn by Robert E. Schultz.

The Campaign against Five Points Brothels

Although a triangle of land containing "horrors too awful to mention" had been cleared at Five Points in 1829, another campaign was mounted in 1850. The original attempt at slum clearance was a reaction against the crowding of residential and commercial structures in "wedges," where modest wooden single-family houses had been converted to accommodate grocers, tavern keepers, and boardinghouse keepers (Blackmar 1989:93). The 1850 campaign targeted brothels. According to Gilfoyle (1992:88, 138, 184), New York City police captain John McManus brought indictments against over 40 brothels at Five Points. McManus had the support of two police court justices, the district attorney, and the future head of the Five Points Mission. There were also plenty of people whose support he did not have, and his effort to extinguish prostitution in the district was not particularly successful. Numerous politicians (for example, Alderman Patrick Kelly, U.S. Marshal Isaiah Rynders, Congressman John Clancy) in mid-nineteenth-century New York derived political support from the proprietors of brothels and depended on those same proprietors for regular payments in return for protection from the police. The police themselves were often in reciprocal relationships with madams, who paid them on a regular basis to leave their establishments alone. Police salaries were low, and brothel bribes provided much-appreciated income.

It was also true that some of the most successful establishments at Five Points were owned by members of elite families who didn't want to lose the rental income. These wealthy men bought old buildings and granted long-term leases to entrepreneurial merchants, brokers, and shopkeepers, who sublet them to other tenants. In other words, a man like John Livingston, brother of Chancellor Robert R. Livingston, one of the nation's founding fathers, did not directly rent to prostitutes: his lease holder did. Livingston had begun buying land around Paradise Square at the heart of the Five Points in 1800. By 1828 he controlled at least five brothels on Anthony Street near Paradise Square; between 1820 and 1850, he owned more than thirty.

McManus' attack on the brothels, as well as the effort to widen Anthony Street, had everything to do with the neighborhood's reputation as a den of iniquity. McManus was a reformer and really believed prostitution was an evil that could be eliminated. The street crusaders were men of means who wanted to ensure their own property values to the west by getting rid of the boisterous street life in the adjacent neighborhood (Blackmar 1989:176). By this time Five

Points was famous as the center of the city's lowlife and had become a tourist at-traction. Charles Dickens' visit in 1841 solidified this reputation and even gave New York a kind of legitimacy as a city worthy of comparison to the great cities of Europe. Prostitution, it seems, was part of what made a nineteenth-century city truly urban. Considered in that context, Five Points was at the forefront, along with Corlear's Hook and Water Street, where brothels had thrived since after the Revolutionary War. By 1850, when McManus mounted his campaign at Five Points, there were plenty more brothels and saloons uptown.

A City of Sex for Sale

Brothels lined Chapel (called Laurens north of Canal) and Church (called Greene north of Canal) Streets. There were more on Crosby Street and on lower Broadway around New York Hospital (Gilfoyle 1992, 33; Figure 3.2). Broadway between Canal and Houston Streets had been a promenade for prostitutes from the early decades of the nineteenth century onward. Well dressed and in groups of two or three, attractive young women paraded along the avenue that was considered the most fashionable in mid-century New York. Walt Whit-man called it a "mart for prostitutes," where one might find "a notorious cour-tesan taking a respectable promenade in the afternoon" or "a tawdry, hateful, foul-tongued, and harsh voiced harlot" after dark (Gilfoyle 1992:30). Moralist Ned Buntline focused on the latter, describing them as

> poor, painted, tinseled creatures, now pausing before the large windowed hotels to show themselves to the cigar smoking loungers who occupied the big arm chairs within, then smiling with a faint and sickly smile upon some country looking promenader, thus throwing out a bait to induce him to turn aside at the next street corner to speak to them, or to make him follow them to the theater of their nightly infamy. (Buntline 1848:9)

The hotels built along Broadway in the 1830s and 1840s were centers for col-lecting clients, but so were theaters, where many of the lower-class prostitutes did business in what was called the "third tier."

Guides for strangers from out of town described more upscale establish-ments. *The Directory to the Seraglios in New York, Philadelphia, Boston, and All the Principal Cities in the Union,* by Free Loveyer (1859), for instance, de-scribes 67 brothels and assignation houses, plus listing about 20 more. While the book is supposedly a review of respectable houses, it is more accurately a book of advertisements. The opening page notes that any hotel hackman will be able to lead a gentleman to the "fashionable houses herein referred to." Almost all of the 67 brothels described in the guide are portrayed as classy establishments, presumably meant for a middle- or upper-class clientele. The first ad is for Mrs. Leslie's at No. 44 Green Street. It was, supposedly, "one of the most fashionable houses in the city . . . in a respectable quiet neighborhood in the central part of the city . . . a beautiful mansion, elegantly fitted up." The "boarders," the ad says, are "very young, very beautiful, gay and accomplished and cannot be surpassed for sociality and refinement and adhere strictly to the rules of etiquette and society." Also mentioned is the availability of the "very best imported wines" (Loveyer 1859:1). There is little variation in the ads that follow. The boarders are invariably young, beautiful, and accomplished. Some are charming and from the sunny South; others are handsome and agreeable. Miss Lizzie Wright's boarders at No. 665 Houston Street included "several French belles, who attract great attention from the planters of the sunny South" (Loveyer 1859:10). Miss Landon at 54 Leonard Street offered "12 beautiful and charming lady boarders who are furnished with separate apartments elegantly furnished," and Miss Cade at No. 19 Frankford Street kept a place on the "German order with barroom attached" and six very pretty German girls. Mrs. Hathaway at No. 90 Broadway apparently catered to visiting Philadelphians, who would "do well to give this house a call to partake of its wines and view some of their fair Quakeresses from home" (Loveyer 1859:21). Wine is always mentioned and, in rare cases, champagne.

Writing in the middle of the nineteenth century, Walt Whitman believed that "nineteen out of twenty of the mass of American young men, who live in or visit the great cities, are more or less familiar with houses of prostitution and are customers to them" (from On Vice, *Brooklyn Daily Times*, in Holloway 1921:6). In the same article, Whitman went on to say that "for the best classes of men under forty years of age, living in New York and Brooklyn, the mechanics, apprentices, sea faring men, drivers of horses, butchers, machinists, etc., the custom is to go among prostitutes as an ordinary thing. Nothing is thought of it—or rather the wonder is, how there can be any 'fun' without it" (Holloway 1921:6). While Whitman was not a moralist (or in any sense opposed to sex), he did worry about venereal disease, which he called the "bad disorder." Because suffering from venereal disease was so universally kept secret, he thought it would result in a generation of "scrofulous growth of children, dropsies, feebleness, premature death, and suffering" (Holloway 1921:6). Others worried more about moral contagion. In *The Secrets of the Great City,* Martin (later known as James McCabe [1882]) wrote, "Society is corrupt to its very heart in the great city and there are thousands of nominally virtuous women who lead, in secret, lives of shame" (Martin 1868:285).

A Five Points Brothel on the Inside

The primary documentary research conducted for the Courthouse site did not uncover the expected record of poverty and vice that yellow journalists portrayed (Ingle et al. 1990). Even the profile of residents drawn from census records did not fit with the presumed population of Five Points. In 1855, for which there is detailed occupational information in the New York State census, 25% (133) of the residents of the block who listed occupations were laborers, while 15.7% (84 women and 35 men) were in the clothing trades (tailors, clothiers, tailoresses, seamstresses, dressmakers, capmakers, and milliners), and 6% were shoemakers (15). Another 5% were involved in construction in one way or another (for example, carpenters, bricklayers, masons, plasterers, painters, glass cutters, roofers, surveyors), and 6% were servants. In addition to various artisans (blacksmith, dyer, weaver, frame maker, etc.) were 37 clerks, 15 storekeepers, four teachers, one student, a Methodist minister, and two policemen (New York State Census 1855).

The artifacts recovered from various mid-nineteenth-century households didn't suggest dire poverty either. There were sets of dishes and even serving pieces (albeit in the least expensive patterns available), matching glass tablewares, a variety of medicines and cosmetics, personal possessions (including smoking pipes, pocketknives, and umbrella parts), decorative figurines and flowerpots, scraps of cloth from the sewing trades, and plenty of pins, needles, and buttons. Meat—mainly pork, beef, and lamb—was eaten by most households, and there was lots of fish. Rather than reflecting poverty, the artifacts from these properties suggested families striving for respectability and taking advantage of the commercial goods and foodstuffs available in the city. One assemblage, however, stood out as being different. The artifacts recovered from a privy at 10/12 Orange Street were more expensive.

Among the costly artifacts was a complete tea-and-coffee set made of Chinese Export porcelain (Figure 3.3). The set included nine-inch plates, a slop bowl, a tea caddy, handled coffee cups, and handle-less teacups/bowls with

Figure 3.3. Chinese Export enameled porcelain coffee and tea set, early nineteenth century, found in the brothel privy (Feature AG). Courthouse site, Lower Manhattan, New York City.

elegant overglaze decoration. Wine was apparently the drink of choice: 100 wine bottles were recovered, plus 65 tumblers. There was also an unusual number of cup plates (14), the small plates that are sometimes used as coasters or for the small snacks served in saloons and brothels. One set displayed an unlikely decoration of cows standing in a grove of trees. The recovered food remains suggested two levels of consumption—expensive and much less so. Among the expensive foods found were veal, beef short loin, mutton loin, and rack of mutton, as well as soft-shell clams and salmon (Milne and Crabtree 2001:36–37). Not one of these foods was found in the features associated with other households. The cheapest cuts of meat—picnic hams and pork foreshank/hocks—and quantities of inexpensive fish, however, made up the largest portion of food remains from the brothel. There was also a dichotomy in the dishes found. Besides the fancy porcelain tea/coffee set and several other elegant tea sets were the same everyday dinner dishes being used in the nearby tenements. They were characteristically decorated in the shell-edge and willow patterns and included many serving dishes (17), platters (5), and pitchers (24).

In 1843 an indictment was brought against John Donohue for his "common, ill-governed, and disorderly house" in the cellar of 12 Orange Street (*State ex rel. Blackall et al. v. Donohue* 1843). The indictment was brought by an Irish-born tinsmith named Edward Blackall at 12½ Orange Street and storekeeper Robert J. Gordon of 10 Orange, before George W. Matsell, a police justice on the city's police court. It described the disorderly house as "a rest for prostitutes and others of ill name and fame, where great numbers of characters are in the nightly practice of reveling until late and improper hours of the night, dancing, drinking, carousing to a great disgrace of the neighborhood." What it did not describe was what life was like for the prostitutes who lived and worked inside. The artifacts recovered dated to the same period as the indictment, and the archaeologists speculated that they were thrown out when the brothel was closed down.

The Orange Street brothel sounds like the German type described by Dr. William Sanger (1939:560), although the named owner, John Donohue, was Irish and apparently managed many properties along this block of Orange Street in the 1840s. What made 10/12 Orange Street fit Sanger's German type was the fact that it was attached to a basement saloon and was surrounded by German shops. The artifact assemblage was distinctive, not because of its ethnic associations, but because of the combination of things that related to the private lives of women and to public entertaining at a fancier level than was suggested by artifact assemblages found on neighboring lots. There was also evidence that the women at 10/12 Orange busied themselves with sewing when they weren't working. The contents of an excavated sewing box included the usual hooks, eyes, and straight pins, plus a carved bone stiletto for putting decorative holes or patterning in embroidery, a delicate small thimble, a folding copper-alloy and wood ruler, and a thread winder made out of a bone lice comb that had its teeth removed (Griggs 2000:295; Figure 3.4). The tiny, double knob-shaped objects made out of bone recovered were identified as the tops of lace bobbins, and there were also beads of different colors (blue, black, clear, and green) to go with them. Bobbins were weighted at the bottom with a ring of beads known as the spangle.

Although Dr. William Sanger had thought most prostitutes idled away their free time reading novels, he did admit to seeing two or three girls in the "reception room for a German brothel knitting or sewing" (1939:560). It is doubtful that he visited No. 10/12 Orange Street, but the sewing box contents demonstrate that the women there busied themselves productively while waiting for the working part of the day to begin. They also probably did their real eating before their work began. Meals of ham or fish, potatoes, and vegetables passed on big white platters would have made it difficult to do anything but nibble delicately at the fancy foods that were served to clients later.

Except for buttons, there was scant evidence of the women's clothing. One

Figure 3.4. Sewing assemblage associated with the Orange Street brothel (Feature AG).

was a single piece of cloth that might have belonged to a dress—a fragment of wool that had lost its color (artifact inventory, Feature AG, Yamin, ed. 2000, vol. IV). The only other cloth was a small piece attached to a bit of metal. There were many outer-garment buttons made of bone (38) and 19 made of a copper alloy. Undergarment buttons (18) were all made of bone. The only possibly fancy buttons, all for outer garments, were mother of pearl (2) and shell (7). Hooks (11) and eyes (10) relate to female clothing but not to its details. Shoes were not described in the artifact inventory and could not be reexamined, because the artifacts from the privy were tragically lost in the September 11, 2001, attack on Lower Manhattan, which destroyed the building where the collection had been analyzed and was temporarily stored. Artifacts associated with grooming included combs made of bone and tortoise shell, a hairbrush and a toothbrush, and many fragments of mirrors. The only piece of jewelry recovered was a copper-alloy and shell pendant; fan parts were made of bone.

In spite of the lack of artifacts associated with personal identity, the archaeological remains associated with the brothel reveal a picture of life that is unavailable from the documentary record. Helen Jewett, whose life as a prostitute in this period has been vividly described in the book *Their Sisters' Keepers* (Hill 1993), undoubtedly enjoyed a more elegant lifestyle in the upscale brothel she lived in on Thomas Street than the prostitutes at 10/12 Orange Street, but the archaeological evidence suggests that they, too, used *things* to create a respectable environment for their customers and for themselves. They may even have chosen ceramics to please their customers. Commodore McDonnough's War of 1812 victory over the British Navy at the Battle of Champlain is portrayed on a dark blue transfer-printed cup and small plate, and there is also a pitcher emblazoned with the seal of the United States (Brighton 2000:B-15; Figure 3.5). Perhaps individual prostitutes displayed these masculine-themed items in their rooms, or maybe they were part of the decor of the common room.

Helen Jewett was murdered by a client in 1836, a crime that got sensational coverage in the press and gained a certain kind of fame for Jewett, while the Orange Street prostitutes worked in anonymity. Their work, however, does not seem so different from that in the upscale establishments described in the guide to the seraglios (Loveyer 1859) discussed above or even at Rosina

Figure 3.5. Cup and saucer decorated with the American Commemorative pattern: "Commodore McDonnough's Victory," dark blue transfer print, Enoch Wood and Sons (ca. 1824–1835). From brothel privy (Feature AG).

Townsend's City Hotel, where Helen Jewett lived. They all faced the same dangers to their health and to their incomes (prostitutes needed youth to prosper). The medicine bottles associated with the Orange Street brothel (a total of 39) suggest that the resident prostitutes had access to a physician or dispensary. Almost 80% of the bottles (35) were the ethical type that could be obtained only with a doctor's prescription, while just 21% were the patent type that were sold commercially as cure-alls (Bonasera 2000:373; Brighton 2008). While the number of bottles does not suggest an alarmingly sick household, the two glass urinals recovered suggest something else (Figure 3.6). The urinals, made espe-

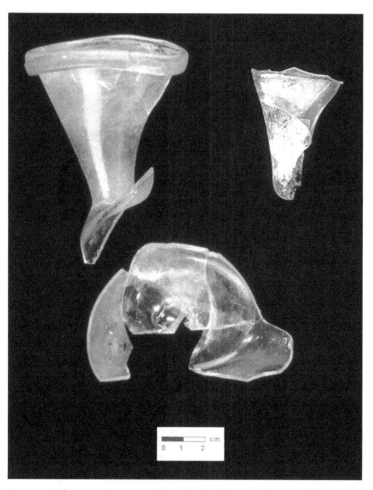

Figure 3.6. Glass urinals recovered from the brothel privy. (Feature AG).

cially for women, were probably used by prostitutes when they were confined to bed with venereal disease, which was rampant in the population. William Sanger reported that nearly half the prostitutes in New York at the time of his study (1858) suffered from syphilis (Sanger 1939:676). There was also the ever-present fear of unwanted pregnancies. Only one syringe was found in the brothel assemblage, although the six copper cent coins found may have been used to cover the cervix (Yamin 2005:10). The copper supposedly made the vagina less conducive to sperm survival.

It is somewhat surprising that more syringes were not present in the brothel assemblage, although several came from privies on other properties. Douching was used for a number of purposes (cleansing, contraception, treatment for female ailments) and was popular by the middle of the nineteenth century (Geiger 2013). Geiger, who studied syringes recovered from City Hall Park in New York City, speculates that syringes may have been missing from brothel assemblages because they were so valuable to women. "If a prostitute earned enough only to adopt a middle-class front," Geiger speculates, "she might retain her personal items more closely rather than discard them into trash deposits as more wealthy households did" (2013:20).

There were obviously ways to prevent pregnancy in this time period, but there were also babies born. The toys and moralizing china found in the Orange Street brothel assemblage attest to the presence of children. Parts from two children's tea sets plus part of a doll and nine marbles were recovered. Among the several child-size cups found was one inscribed with a sentimental message about a loving grandmother (Yamin 2000:139).

More unsettling was the evidence suggesting infanticide. The neonatal skeletal remains of two full-term individuals and the partial remains of a third were recovered from the brothel privy (Crist 2005). There was no evidence of trauma on either of the full-term infants. According to physical anthropologist Thomas Crist's analysis, they died near the time of birth. Their bones were found mingled with baby pig bones, possibly in an effort to conceal them (Crist 2005:19). Infanticide was practiced by both married and unmarried women, and archaeological evidence of infanticide has been found elsewhere. In Philadelphia, for instance, the skeletal remains of two infants, one a full-term newborn and the other a seven-month fetus, were found between two trash deposits in a privy dating to the eighteenth century. The privy was associated with the Pine Street Friends Meeting House, but the trash may have originated off site (Burnston 1982:154). Just as in the New York case, the infant bones were mixed with animal bones, most of which came from meals. It appears that prostitutes were not alone in wanting to conceal the evidence of infanticide.

Prostitution could not have been an easy way to make a living in the middle of the nineteenth century, albeit a more lucrative one than other jobs available to women. While published sources have described prostitutes as companions for men as well as sexual partners (for example, Hill 1993), the archaeological assemblage brings to life the companionship among the women. They apparently spent time sewing, probably in one another's company. It is possible to envision the prostitutes passing daytime hours sewing and chatting while birds sang in their cages (bird-watering devices were recovered). Not unlike middle-class women in this period, they undoubtedly exchanged intimacies, shared problems, and transferred knowledge. Carroll Smith-Rosenberg's (1985) study of several middle-class women's letters in the mid-nineteenth century reveals the kinds of intimate relationships that women had with one another. She proposes that "rigid gender role differentiation within family and society" led to the emotional segregation of men and women and that "the biological realities of frequent pregnancies, childbirth, nursing, and menopause bound women together in physical and emotional intimacy" (Smith-Rosenberg 1985:59–60). While we don't have any documented correspondence between prostitutes for this period, it is not unreasonable to think that they, too, depended on one another for support. The interviews with Storyville prostitutes in Al Rose's book about that notorious red-light district in New Orleans in the late nineteenth and early twentieth centuries reveal various kinds of intimacy. In one instance a prostitute remembers losing her virginity alongside another young girl with whom she worked as a pair (Rose 1974:150). Another describes eating a meal at three or four in the afternoon on a round table in the kitchen and "talking like young girls" (Rose 1974:163). Although most of Bellocq's (1976) famous photographs of Storyville show women alone, one is of two women sitting on the floor playing cards and sharing a bottle of some kind of alcohol.

Camaraderie among prostitutes in the brothels of Storyville may be well documented, but the image of it in a Five Points brothel is a surprise. Mr. McManus' attacks on the Five Points brothels in 1850 would not have taken into account the gentility suggested by the artifacts. He, like so many others, could see only evil at Five Points, while brothels were thriving all over the city at mid-century. Five Points brothels—or at least some of them—were surely no worse than the acceptable ones uptown, but it was the downtown ones that

were under attack. One wonders if the payoffs to the police were not as gener-
ous downtown and the houses therefore not worth keeping in business. Or
perhaps, it was simply that attacking the lower sort was more acceptable than
attacking the well heeled.

Prostitutes and Self-Respect

New York City's antebellum prostitutes, it appears, were more concerned with
economic survival than with either their health or morals. While bourgeois
men and women saw young women who turned to prostitution as falling into
ruin, the women themselves saw prostitution as salvation from economic ruin
(Stansell 1987:175). "For the widowed mother, the downwardly mobile jour-
neyman, and the poor immigrant, prostitution was not a violation of moral
propriety but a necessary part of the household economy" (Gilfoyle 1992:66).
Historian Timothy Gilfoyle speculates that 5 to 10% of all young nineteenth-
century women in New York between the ages of 15 and 30 prostituted themselves at some point. The numbers vary. Whether or not prostitutes felt degraded by commercial sex is an open question, but they surely felt degraded
by work that did not offer a living wage. The *National Laborer* estimated that
women's pay in 1836 was no more than 37.5 cents a day, and in 1845 it was
merely $2.00 a week (Gilfoyle 1992:59).

Dr. William Sanger's study of prostitutes at Blackwell's Island in 1859 found
that the majority of his interviewees came from families headed by men who
practiced middling or petty bourgeois professions, including 22% who were
farmers and 31% who were skilled artisans. The greatest predictor of prostitution was not ethnicity, birthplace, or even class, but rather the death of a
parent, especially the father (Gilfoyle 1992:66, citing Sanger 1939). Many accounts suggest that the acquisition of fancy clothing was a reason to prostitute
oneself. Besides parading on Broadway, prostitutes attended fancy-dress balls
alongside respectable bourgeois wives and were virtually indistinguishable
from their married counterparts. They dressed for men, but they also dressed
for themselves.

Historian Christine Stansell (1987) has also made the important point that
besides clothing, young New Yorkers wanted to be free of their families and
free to use their incomes on themselves instead of having to contribute to
family upkeep. They may have told Sanger that prostitution was a choice
because they wanted to shock him, but it is more likely that they said it be-

cause, above all, they did not want to seem like pathetic victims. They saw themselves as agents in their own lives.

Class and the Institution of Prostitution

Class played a role on many levels. Reformers focused on eliminating prostitution in lower-class neighborhoods, where they could claim moral superiority. Women, as well as men, condemned prostitutes for living lives of depravity, but women also saw prostitution as something else. "The friendless prostitute," according to historian Carroll Smith-Rosenberg, "symbolized . . . their own powerlessness within the new urban economy" (1985:45–46). A small group of women in New York City organized something called the Female Moral Reform Society with the goal of converting prostitutes to Evangelical Protestantism and closing the city's brothels. The society also "hoped to confront the larger and more fundamental abuse, the double standard, and the male sexual license it condoned" (Smith-Rosenberg 1985:109). While these women, and other women reformers as well, surely saw themselves as superior to the prostitutes they were attempting to rescue, they put at least some of the blame for their state on the men who were their clients and went so far as to station themselves across the street from brothels to record male clients who entered (Smith-Rosenberg 1985:113).

That prostitution also thrived in upscale neighborhoods was harder to confront and not part of an ideology that required (and assumed) that members of the middle class, both men and women, were expected to conform to middle-class values, that is, the "cult of domesticity." Just as they did not see variations among the poor, the reformers do not seem to have appreciated how class was being manipulated by the prostitutes themselves. The archaeological record of the brothel in the heart of Five Points suggests that most of the prostitutes at 10/12 Orange probably came from the working class; nevertheless, they knew how to appeal to a middle-class clientele. They knew how to use material things and manners to make a living for themselves from the indulgences of the men who were willing to pay for their company. And they knew as well as their middle-class sisters that material things could be used to convey messages about class. If there is a basic premise in historical archaeology, it is that objects—the stuff we dig up—are loaded with meaning, much of it related to the expression of class, ethnicity, and gender (see, for example, Rotman 2009). The problem is to interpret the meaning, not always a straightforward task. If class is always complicated (Wurst and Fitts

1999:1), it is even more complicated when symbols are being manipulated in unconventional ways. At Five Points, working-class prostitutes played at looking middle class to appeal to their clients, probably to make their clients more comfortable in an era when men expected their women to be subservient and demure.

In the heart of Washington, DC, however, the clients were men of wealth and power—a higher class of clients than those at Five Points—and the capital parlor houses set the stage with champagne and fine dining for prostitutes presenting high-class hospitality.

Working Women in the Nation's Capital City

Two neighborhoods west of Capitol Hill and along the Washington Canal (modern Constitution Avenue) were known for prostitution and other extralegal activities in the nineteenth century. The Island, site of Mary Ann Hall's first-class brothel, was in an area separated from the rest of the city by the Washington Canal and bordered by the Potomac River (Figure 3.7). The historic Island now includes the National Mall (occupied by several Smithsonian museums) and several blocks of government office buildings south of the National Mall. In the mid-nineteenth century, the Island was home to numerous brothels in addition to Hall's, as well as the gas holder of the Washington Gas Light Company, a foundry, an oyster house, working-class family households, and the Smithsonian Institution's first building, the Castle, completed in 1855 (Boschke 1861; Sachse 1852; Seifert et al. 2000:116, 124).

The second neighborhood known for prostitution in the nineteenth century was called Hooker's Division. It was located north of the Island and was bounded by Fifteenth Street, NW; Pennsylvania Avenue; and the Washington Canal (Figure 3.8). The area is now the west end of modern Federal Triangle and Constitution Avenue, which overlies the filled Washington Canal. Major General Joseph Hooker, commander of the Army of the Potomac, addressed the issue of carousing soldiers occupying the capital city by concentrating the city's prostitutes south of Pennsylvania Avenue (Cheek and Seifert 1994:271; see also Green 1962 1:251; Leech 1941:264). Local news stories in Washington's *Evening Star* (for example, 29 August 1864:3; 2 March 1865:3; 19 March 1865:329) refer to the neighborhood as Hooker's Division: the place to find the men of Hooker's Division during their off-duty hours (James O. Hall, personal communication 1989). The use of the term "hooker" for a prostitute appears to

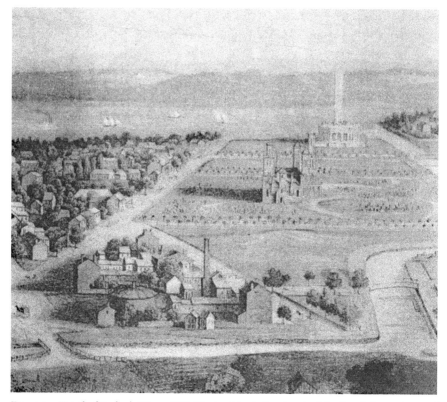

Figure 3.7. Detail of Sachse's *View of Washington* (1852) showing the Island and the environs of Mary Ann Hall's brothel. Hall's house is the tall building in the lower left (southeast) corner of the image. The Smithsonian Castle is in the center of the image.

predate the designation of the Division (Press 1984:56), but the double entendre of Hooker's Division probably helped popularize the term.

During the Civil War, the provost marshal conducted a survey of brothels, which listed more than 30 brothels in Hooker's Division and 20 south of the canal, on the Island. The remaining 20 brothels on the list were scattered around the city (USACE 1864–1865). The number of brothels and prostitutes had increased dramatically with the general population of Washington, DC, during the war. Thousands of soldiers were brought to the capital to staff the Circle Forts that protected the city. Others waited there for orders or were being treated for battle wounds or disease contracted in military encampments. Government bureaucrats, businessmen and con men, and freed and escaped slaves also came to the capital city. Madams and prostitutes followed to take

Figure 3.8. Detail of Boschke's *Topographical Map of the District of Columbia Surveyed in the Years 1856, '57, '58, and '59* (1861). The archaeological excavations in Hooker's Division were on the north side of Ohio Avenue. Hall's house is on the southwest corner of the block bounded by Maine Avenue, the Washington Canal, and Maryland Avenue.

advantage of the huge increase in the market for their services. In the major eastern cities—and even midwestern cities—madams closed their local houses to open new ones in Washington, DC (O'Brien 2005:50, citing Leech 1941:261). In 1863 the *Evening Star* newspaper estimated that there were 5,000 prostitutes working in brothels or as streetwalkers (Lowry 1994:68).

The Geography of Vice

General Hooker is given credit for segregating the brothels to facilitate military surveillance; however, several factors appear to have reinforced the concentration of brothels in Hooker's Division (Porter-Lupu 2016:3–4). The area along the Washington Canal, the most unpleasant part of the city center, was undesirable for residential occupation because of its low elevation. Its central location, however, was convenient for Capitol Hill politicians and bureaucrats. The low elevation of the area meant that it was within a direct sightline between the White House and Capitol Hill, but only building roofs could actually be seen from the higher elevations, and the blocks included narrow alleys, making it possible for clients and prostitutes to move about without attracting notice.

Both the Island and Hooker's Division were conveniently located a short walk from the halls of power: the Capitol, Treasury, and White House. By the end of the nineteenth century, most of the houses in Hooker's Division were brothels. Brothels persisted through the nineteenth century in Washington, DC, as extralegal business operations. Fornication was illegal, but in 1914 Congress passed the Kenyon Act, which made operating or owning a house for the purpose of prostitution in the federal district a public nuisance (CDC 1914:359–361).

The Capital Parlor House

Nineteenth-century descriptions of high-class brothels in Washington, DC, are consistent with William Sanger's 1858 descriptions of the parlor house type. John B. Ellis's 1869 *The Sights and Secrets of the National Capitol* reports that such houses were patronized by "men high in public life," such as military officers, lawyers, doctors, and state governors (1869:458–459). Hall's house on the Island and those in Hooker's Division enjoyed the ideal location for such visitors.

The brothels in downtown Washington, DC, afforded their working women some professional opportunities unique to the national capital: prostitutes and madams had special access to lawmakers and were thought to promote certain proposed legislation with important visitors. For their efforts, these professional women were rewarded by those who would benefit from said legislation. In his *Mysteries and Miseries of America's Great Cities,* James Buel describes prostitutes in the Senate's ladies' audience chamber balcony, who "became objects of unctuous admiration, displaying to excellent advantage their gorgeous apparel with half revealing monuments of maternity peeping over brilliant bodices" (1883:180).

Another peculiar aspect of the business in Washington, DC, was that it was seasonal work. The city's population rose substantially when Congress was in session, and most Congressmen came to town without their families and took lodgings for the session. During the summer, anyone who could leave town did.

Welcome to Mary Ann Hall's First-Class Brothel on the Island

Mary Ann Hall owned and operated one of the finest and best-known brothels in nineteenth-century Washington, DC. She began her career as a prostitute, but she was clearly not taking the first step on the road to ruin, but rather her path to prosperity. When she died in 1886 at the age of 71, her assets, valued at nearly $90,000, included a well-furnished, three-story brick brothel in downtown Washington, DC, and a 72-acre farm in Virginia overlooking the capital city (O'Brien 2005:47).

Hall built her large house at 349 Maryland Avenue (DCTB 1840) in 1840, when she was in her early twenties (USBC 1840, 1850). The 1840 federal census lists her as head of a household including four other white women in their twenties; a free African American woman in her late twenties or early thirties; and a young male slave. Hall is not listed as keeping a brothel, nor is any occupant listed as a prostitute. The members of the household appear unrelated (each with a different surname), thus, not members of a family household. The household was probably functioning as a brothel with four prostitutes and two African American household servants.

During the 1840s Mary Ann Hall made significant improvements to the property, evidenced by a doubling in its value by the 1850 tax assessment. Her personal property also increased in value during the same period. By the 1850 census, Hall's occupation is listed as a 33-year-old "substitute." Other occupants of the house included Hall's 31-year-old sister Elizabeth, a 22-year-old woman (also listed as a substitute), and 33-year-old Elizabeth Lowe, an ex-substitute. A free mulatto woman, Judy Fleet, served as housekeeper (USBC 1850). Later census documents list women in Hall's household as prostitutes, so we understand "substitute" to be a gloss for prostitute (that is, a temporary substitute for a wife).

The 1864 provost marshal's list of bawdy houses included Hall's house as a Class 1 brothel with 18 resident prostitutes (USACE 1864–1865). Most houses on the list included several resident prostitutes, but Hall's was by far the largest. Her business was clearly prospering, and the value of her real estate had increased to $10,000 (DCTB 1864).

Hall's house was high-class, but that did not mean the house and its resident prostitutes escaped notice of the press or the police. In 1862 the *Evening Star* reported the theft of a hack carrying police officers that was driven to "Miss Hall's establishment on the Island." The hack and team were recovered in nearby Tin Cup Alley, along with two suspects (O'Brien 2005:51 citing *Evening Star* 1862). The *Evening Star* in 1863 reported that several of the prostitutes who requested a federal escort to Richmond, Virginia, the Confederacy's capital, were from "Mary Hall's" (O'Brien 2005, citing Leech 1941:265). Of those who stayed, some clearly voiced their support for the Confederacy: Annie Smith, Alice Martin, and Cora Wilbraham, "three fallen angels sojourning at Mary Hall's hades," were detained by a mounted provost guard after singing the *Bonnie Blue Flag* and shouting for Jefferson Davis from their carriage. The three were released after payment of a fine (O'Brien 2005:51, citing *Evening Star* 12 March 1863).

Mary Ann Hall's house and other high-class brothels were raided in January 1864. Hall was indicted for running a bawdy house, and her trial was held in February. The *Evening Star* covered the trial, reporting that Hall's brothel "has had—it is no exaggeration to say—a national reputation for the last quarter century, and the fact that the business concerns of this 'old and well-established house' were being overhauled in Court has really attracted considerable attention to the case" (O'Brien 2005:52, citing *Evening Star* 1864). Witnesses included several police officers and detectives who had been called to remove disruptive patrons or to investigate various crimes in the city. Clearly, these law-enforcement professionals had known the business of Hall's house; yet court documents do not suggest actions were taken to close the house. The defense attorney called witnesses whose testimony was designed to support the argument that Hall's residence was her house in Virginia, which had been occupied by Union troops since 1862. Hall was found guilty, but the *Evening Star* did not report the consequences of the verdict (O'Brien 2005:52, citing *Evening Star* 1864). It is unlikely that Hall was incarcerated; more likely, she was fined—the common result of a guilty verdict, which was considered a cost of doing business.

After the end of the Civil War, Mary Ann Hall's house continued to prosper, probably owing to its reputation and proximity to Capitol Hill. Although the soldiers had left town, many prostitutes continued to live and work on the Island and in Hooker's Division (USBC 1870, 1880). The Island also included dwellings occupied by families and prostitutes in the same buildings. Other clandestine activities were common, including selling liquor without a license and fencing stolen goods. The neighboring Shea family rented rooms to prostitutes and appears to have been involved in all such activities—as well as murder: Maria Shea shot a policeman when he confronted her about a stolen watch. Shea was acquitted, claiming the gun discharged accidentally, although the *Evening Star* cited witnesses who claimed to have heard her say that she would "blow [the officer's] brains out" and "cut his heart out" (O'Brien 2005:53, citing *Evening Star* 1871). A Shea family descendant read about the archaeological investigations on the Island and this story about Maria Shea. The descendant contacted JMA's office to say that the story passed down in the family was that Maria shot a black man who tried to steal something from her. The descendant concluded that critical details of the family version of the story had been altered. Despite the Shea family's questionable business practices—or, perhaps, because of them—the family prospered and purchased and improved several lots on the Island in the 1870s and 1880s (O'Brien 2005:53 citing USBC 1870, 1880, 1900; DCTB 1876–1879; DCBP 1877–1926 [1878]; DCGA 1886–1934; Sanborn Map Company 1888; Hopkins 1887).

By the 1870s Hall appears to have been living in Virginia (as she claimed in 1864), where she was enumerated in the 1870 and 1880 manuscript censuses (USBC 1870, 1880), although city directories list her at her brothel at 349 Maryland Avenue (Boyd 1867, 1868, 1872; Boyd 1885). The house was probably run by a manager listed as a housekeeper (O'Brien 2005:53, citing USBC 1870, 1880; Boyd 1878, 1879, 1881, 1882). The names Emily Hinkerly [or Hewitt] and Elizabeth/Lizzie Peterson appear in court documents, directories, and census records.

Mary Ann Hall became ill in the winter of 1885 and died at 349 Maryland Avenue (not in Virginia) in 1886 (DCSC 1886). Following a private funeral, she was buried next to her mother, Elizabeth, and her sister Catherine in Congressional Cemetery. It is likely that Hall purchased these cemetery lots when her mother died in 1863 (O'Brien 2005:54). Hall's impressive monument was inscribed, "Truth was her motto, charity for all. Dawn is coming" (O'Brien 2005:55). It is the largest figurative monument in Congressional Cemetery (Figure 3.9).

Mary Ann Hall's estate was worth more than $20,000 in real estate and $67,000 in bonds and securities. The room-by-room probate inventory demonstrated that the house at 349 Maryland Avenue was furnished expensively (O'Brien 2005:55, citing DCSC 1886). The size of her estate was known to her two brothers, who sued Mary Ann's surviving sisters, Elizabeth and Lavinia, for a share of the estate. Elizabeth had lived and worked with Mary Ann in the 1850s and 1860s (USBC 1850, 1860), and Lavinia came to Washington, DC, when Mary Ann became ill. In one of the documents in the Hall legal file, there was a line listing Lavinia as the wife of Henry Colton—but the line was struck

Figure 3.9. Mary Ann Hall's monument in the Congressional Cemetery. Photograph by Marc Brodsky.

out and "single" was written over the strikeout (DCSC 1886). The information is worth noting, as Colton was a known brothel keeper in New York (Gilfoyle 1992:47). It appears that brothel-keeping was a Hall family business, at least among the women, and the brothers hoped to profit from their sisters' work (O'Brien 2005:55). Elizabeth and Lavinia each claimed some of the household furnishings. Each of the brothers was awarded $11,000 from the estate, and the sisters divided the remaining money (O'Brien 2005:56, citing DCSC 1886). Hall's Virginia farm was sold in 1888.

The Archaeology of the Island

Mary Ann Hall's story came to light when the land on the National Mall, historically known as the Island, that had included her brothel on Maryland Avenue was selected as the site for the Smithsonian Institution's National Museum of the American Indian. The planning process for the museum building's construction included an assessment of cultural resources that warranted identification, evaluation, and treatment before other ground-disturbing work could begin (Seifert and Balicki 2005:59). Construction of a temporary office building during World War II was thought to have destroyed or damaged remains of previous buildings on the site, but subsurface archaeological testing proved this assumption wrong. There were areas of destruction, but there were also areas of good preservation where remains of several nineteenth-century dwellings were intact. The archaeological evaluation demonstrated that the site could yield data on the family households occupying the dwellings, as well as the large, three-story brick building that was identified in many documents as Mary Ann Hall's brothel.

The excavations included the testing of two historic lots, Lot 11 and Lot 12. In the mid-nineteenth century, Lot 11 was undeveloped, but Mary Ann Hall's brothel, on the adjacent Lot 12, was the only nearby occupied lot. Only architectural remains were found on Lot 12, but refuse on the yard surface and midden deposits next door on Lot 11 appeared to be associated with the brothel. These deposits, which dated to the 1860s, were sealed beneath a ca. 1871 fill layer confidently attributed to a well-documented municipal construction project (Seifert et al. 1998:143; USC 1874:253).

Analysis of functional groups (an analytical approach described in chapter 2) was used for gross-level comparison of the artifact assemblages from Mary Ann Hall's house and the neighboring family households. Then certain groups thought to shed light on brothel households were examined more closely. For example, only in the brothel assemblages did clothing artifacts amount to more than 1% of the total. These artifacts, including buttons and shoes, suggest that greater expenditures were made on personal attire by brothel inmates as compared to residents of family households. There were few personal items—mirror fragments, hairpins and combs, jewelry—in the brothel assemblage, perhaps because these objects were owned by individual prostitutes, who took them along when they left.

Artifacts in the activities group, mostly flowerpot sherds and lamp-chimney glass, accounted for nearly 2% of the brothel assemblage, a higher percentage than in family households. These artifacts suggest attention to genteel decor and the lighting necessary for night work.

Hall's white ironstone dishes and porcelain tablewares and teawares produced the highest mean ceramic index value of all the Washington brothels. The index value, which indicates relative cost of the ceramics when purchased, was higher than index values for all neighboring working- and middle-class households, suggesting that more was spent on expensive dishes in the brothel than in the family households. Hall's teawares included several white, paneled cups and saucers in the gothic style that was popular in middle-class households, where the style was interpreted as a reflection of Christian values and the cult of domesticity. In the brothel this style may have been meant to evoke a genteel environment (Seifert and Balicki 2005:66).

Evidence for the food on the table also documents household expenditures. The inmates of Hall's brothel and their clients enjoyed domestic meat, as well as wild birds, turtle, and fish, suggesting that the household was able to purchase a variety of specialty foods and delicacies at local markets, as well as beef, pork, and mutton/goat of primarily high- to medium-priced cuts. Faunal data also indicate that laying hens were kept on Hall's property. Neighboring working-class households consumed a less varied diet, mostly chicken and pork. Plant foods consumed in the brothel included raspberry, strawberry, fig, grape, apple, cherry/plum, elderberry, peach, bean, squash, walnut, and coconut. Less variety in plant foods was found in the family households (Seifert and Balicki 2005:71).

The beverage of choice in Mary Ann Hall's brothel was champagne, a choice consistent with contemporary accounts reporting that champagne was served only in first-class brothels (Sanger 1939:550). Several of the foil seals that cover the cork were legible, all of which indicate that the preferred type was Piper

Heidseick of Rheims, France (Seifert et al. 1998:123; see also Switzer 1974:25). Unfortunately, the archaeological evidence does not reveal the vessels from which the champagne was consumed: few drinking glasses of any kind were identified in the assemblage.

The archaeological and documentary records of Mary Ann Hall's house reveal a large household whose residents and clients enjoyed fine dining: expensive dishes, choice meat cuts, exotic foods, and champagne. The room-by-room probate inventory of Hall's house at 349 Maryland Avenue documents a house furnished with items typical in a middle-class residence, as well as luxury goods, such as Brussels carpets, oil paintings, and mahogany and rosewood furniture (O'Brien 2005:55–56; DCSC 1886). This was a household that spent a lot on dining, comfort, and elegance. No other household in central Washington, DC, for which we have archaeological data was furnished with the class of Mary Ann Hall's house. Archaeological and documentary data on the neighboring family households on the Island, as well as the brothels and family households in Hooker's Division, present a more modest lifestyle. Across the Washington Canal, in Hooker's Division, we see a different picture.

Ellen Starr's Brothel in the Neighborhood Named for General Hooker

Mrs. Ellen Starr purchased the property at No. 62 Ohio Avenue in Hooker's Division in 1864. She had come from Baltimore in 1858, where she was already an established madam. She arranged for her daughter Mrs. Mary Jane Treakle (also known as Mollie Turner) to move from Norfolk, Virginia, to Washington, DC, to run the house as a brothel (James Hall, personal communication 1989; Seifert 1994:149–150). According to the provost marshal's list, the brothel run by Mollie Turner was a Class 1 house with three inmates (USACE 1864–1865; Tidwell 1988:337). Like Mary Ann Hall's family, the Starr family was also in the brothel-and-prostitution business, as another of Mrs. Starr's daughters, Ellen (also known as Nellie Starr, Ella Turner, and Fannie Harrison), was working at No. 62 Ohio Avenue when she was interviewed by the police:

My name is Nellie Starr. My Native place is Baltimore, State of Maryland. I have been in Washington City D.C. since a week before Christmas. I am about nineteen or twenty years of age. I am not married. I have known John Wilkes Booth about three years; he was in the habit of visiting the house where I live kept by Miss Eliza Thomas, No. 62 Ohio Avenue in the City of Washington. The house is one of prostitution. I have never heard him speak unfavorable of the President. I heard him speak of the President as being a good man just as other people did. I do not distinctly recollect how he was dressed, when I last saw him. I think he had on dark clothes. I think he wore a slouch hat. I do not think it is the one shown me by the district attorney. I know nothing more about the case. I know not with whom he associated with, as I have not been on good terms with him for over a year. The last time I seen Mr. Booth was two weeks ago, at the said house. [signed] Nellie Starr, Ellen Starr, Fannie Harrison. (*U.S. v. J. Wilkes Booth* 1865)

Nellie Starr gave her statement on April 15, 1865, the day that President Lincoln died.

In the mid-1860s Hooker's Division included over 30 brothels (USACE 1864–1865), and the neighborhood continued to be occupied by brothels and family households (USBC 1870, 1880). By the 1890s the number of prostitutes in Hooker's Division increased significantly. Near the turn of the century, Hooker's Division changed from a mixed residential-commercial-industrial neighborhood with some brothels to a district of brothels. In fact, several of the brick townhouses built in the 1890s on Ohio Avenue were probably built as brothels—like the one visited by young Joseph Scheele in 1913. Here is his account:

> There was a house off Ohio Avenue I visited with a fighter from New York City staying in a house in Georgetown, D.C. (my cousin's house). This Italian fighter took me (about 13 years old) after a wrestling match around the corner. The match was between a very *famous man* at the time, *Joe Turner* & some man; nobody could beat him. Turner won. The wrestling match was a block on Penn. Ave., a block from 9th Street in a large arena at that time.
>
> The Brothel House was on a street facing East, 3 stories high, six girls, a Madam; all pretty to me. The fighter picked one & took her out of the room to the stairs to the 2nd floor, I guess, as I sat in the living room with a couple of the girls, which gave me a ginger Ale til the fighter came back; we took the trolley on Penn. Ave. home to Georgetown. (Joseph E. Scheele, personal communication 1989; cited in Seifert 1991:82)

Young Joseph Scheele visited the Hooker's Division house shortly before the brothels were closed. Even though the District of Columbia opened a new office building in the neighborhood in 1908, the brothels were not closed until 1914, with the passage of the Kenyon Act (CDC 1914:359–361; Press 1984:68), which made owning or operating a house for the purpose of prostitution a public nuisance.

The Archaeology of Hooker's Division

Archaeological investigations within Hooker's Division were conducted during the redevelopment of Federal Triangle in the early 1990s, 10 years before the excavations at the site of Mary Ann Hall's house on the Island. The Federal Triangle project tested sites associated with working-class family households and brothels occupied in the late nineteenth and early twentieth centuries, later than the archaeological contexts (ca. 1860–1871) excavated at Hall's house on the Island (Cheek et al. 1991). The investigations in Hooker's Division focused on Squares 257 and 258, which included at least two artifact assemblages associated with brothels, one dating to 1870–1890 and the other dating to 1890–1914. The data from the two projects (which were analyzed using the same methods) provided the opportunity to compare brothels at different points in time, as well as different classes of brothels and family households.

All three brothel assemblages (from Hall's brothel and two Hooker's Division brothels) reflect household composition of residents and visiting clients, as well as the dual function of residence and workplace. In nineteenth-century Washington, DC, home and workplace were separate for most family households: work done at home was homework—the work of running a household; wage labor was done at a separate workplace. When the three brothel collections were compared, differences emerged that suggest that household function alone does not account for a distinctive artifact pattern. The percentage of kitchen artifacts from Hall's brothel, for instance, is much higher than in the Hooker's Division brothels (83% compared to about 50%) (Seifert and Balicki 2005:63). There was a higher percentage of food-preparation and storage vessels at Hall's house, and the tablewares were considerably fancier and more expensive than those found in the Hooker's Division collections. Hall's tables were set with porcelain and ironstone dishes—not the less fashionable pearlwares and whitewares still being used in the neighboring family households. The plain and gilt-edged porcelain tableware in Hall's house sets her house apart from all others in the comparative collections. This assemblage, dominated by expensive tablewares and utility wares, is consistent with a large household serving meals to residents as well as evening guests. The dining tables in the later brothels in Hooker's Division were not as fashionably set as were Hall's, but the turn-of-the-century brothels did have more expensive tablewares than the neighboring working-class family households. The later brothels were also serving expensive meat cuts, probably to clients (Seifert and Balicki 2005:66).

By comparing archaeological assemblages from a range of dates (ca. 1860–1914) and along the Washington Canal, south on the Island and north in Hooker's Division, we see that brothel assemblages in Washington, DC, are consistently different from neighboring working-class family households. However, brothels of different time periods and statuses are also different from each other: brothel assemblages are peculiar, but they are peculiar for different time periods and different economic classes (Seifert et al. 2000:124; Seifert and Balicki 2005:71). Archaeological investigations of brothels and saloons in the American frontier have revealed even more differences. The next chapter looks at a range of venues and cultural contexts of prostitution in the American West.

4

Brothels and Prostitution
in the American West

Most Americans who grew up with the popular genre of westerns in fiction, television, and movies have an image of that core institution of the West, the saloon. In that image the saloon is populated by tough cowboys and fancy women with hearts of gold who just served stiff drinks to tough cowboys. Think Miss Kitty in *Gunsmoke*. No, she did not just serve drinks. No woman who cared about her reputation as a lady entered a saloon in nineteenth-century America.

The frontier West of the imagination and of historical fact was overwhelmingly populated by single males engaged in mining, lumbering, or driving livestock. The predominance of prostitutes in mining camps and frontier towns is generally attributed to the shortage of women (meaning wives or women deemed suitable to be wives). In the late nineteenth and early twentieth centuries, it was commonly understood that an unmarried man—or a man living without a wife—needed access to women willing to provide sexual services for money. Sexual release was, in fact, considered a matter of physical health and well-being (Vermeer 2006:32, 40, citing Goldman 1981).

The demographics and social organization of frontier settlements produced a distinct cultural environment—with a great deal of latitude in behavior. This was especially true in the early days of a settlement, when most occupants were independent miners or prospectors and those offering support by selling goods, services, food, and lodging. All sorts of goods and services were in short supply, including available women. Women in frontier settlements enjoyed greater liberty of behavior and were less restricted in movement and association with the residents of the settlement than women in other situations. Like women elsewhere, they did the work of laundry and sewing, but they were also consulted about medical treatment in the absence of trained medical practitioners. It seems likely that this measure of freedom of movement and behavior was an attraction for adventuresome women.

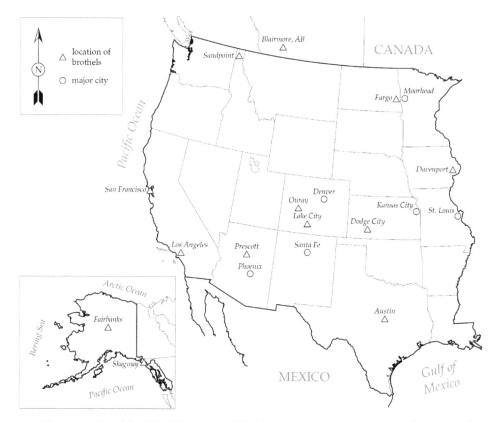

Figure 4.1. Map of the United States west of the Mississippi showing major cities and locations of brothels discussed in the text. Map drawn by Scott Jaquith.

Archaeological investigations designed to understand the work and workplaces of prostitutes in the West are a recent line of inquiry (Figure 4.1). The living and working spaces associated with prostitutes may have been excavated without being recognized, but there is not much evidence that anyone was looking for such sites as a serious research focus until the 1970s.

Archaeologists Look at Prostitution in the West

One of the first archaeologists to consider prostitution in the West was Alexy Simmons (1982, 1989), who developed a model for identifying brothels in the archaeological record of the frontier West from 1860 to 1890. The model relates changes in prostitution to economic and technological variables (1989:137).

The usual sequence of economic phases for mining towns are boom, bonanza, consolidation, recession, and exhaustion; these phases precipitate changes in the settlement patterns of prostitutes (1989:52–53).

The model was tested against five frontier mining town histories or case studies, using documentary sources (Simmons 1989:137), as appropriate archaeological data were not available when she constructed the model (in the 1980s). Simmons found that the lifeways of prostitutes varied depending on status and economic trends and the sociopolitical history of the community (1989:137). In the boom phase, prostitutes were scattered throughout the camp or town, but most were in or near the central commercial district. In the bonanza phase, the settlement pattern was similar, but the population of prostitutes was larger and was working within residential areas. Prostitutes enjoyed the greatest community mobility in these early boom and bonanza phases. In the consolidation phase, regulating ordinances were generally ineffectual, but building fires (attributed to arson) and economic recession were the usual means of segregating prostitution. The recession phase often saw repression as well as segregation (Simmons 1989:139–140).

"Spanish" (Hispanic) prostitutes tended to be aggregated with Euro-American prostitutes, but African American prostitutes were segregated, as were Chinese prostitutes (usually in the local Chinatown). Euro-American men were clients of Chinese prostitutes; Chinese men patronized only Chinese prostitutes (Simmons 1989:138). Chinese prostitutes were generally indentured or enslaved women, not independent practitioners, and their experiences were tied to the economic fortunes of the Chinese community. This structural difference may make Chinese prostitution look different in the archaeological record (Simmons 1989:139).

In Simmons' study, prostitutes are seen as major players in civilizing towns. She argues that prostitutes provided social welfare services and medical care and organized community social events. They also "provided freedom to other women on the frontier by removing the threat of male sexuality and by eroding the nineteenth-century idea of female propriety" (Simmons 1989:140, citing Petrik 1981).

The Special Case of the Chinese Prostitute

Another documentary study addresses Chinese prostitutes in the West. Priscilla Wegars (1993) tells the story of Ah Toy (Ah-Choi), one of the few Chinese women who came to the West as an independent prostitute. Ah Toy arrived in San Francisco in the early 1850s and became the madam of her own brothel in Chinatown.

Most young Chinese women arriving in the West were brought by a *tong* (meaning "hall," a fraternal or secret society) that controlled gambling, opium distribution, or prostitution (Wegars 1993:231). The women brought by the tongs had been sold, kidnapped, or deceived in China with the promise of being married or offered legitimate employment in North America. Most found themselves working as indentured domestic servants or as prostitutes with little control over their daily lives or futures.

The trade in Chinese women was so lucrative in San Francisco that tongs fought with each other for control, sparking the so-called tong wars in the 1870s and 1880s. Alarm over prostitution by Chinese women prompted immigration prohibitions in 1875 designed to prevent the importation of women for the purpose of prostitution. The prohibition made immigration difficult for any Chinese woman, thus increasing the demand for Chinese prostitutes (Wegars 1993:233). There was a hierarchy among Chinese prostitutes, with those considered "high-class" serving only Chinese men. These women lived in comfortable houses, had fine clothing and jewelry, and were permitted to keep gifts given to them by clients. Prostitutes considered "low-class" served anyone who could pay (Chinese or not). These women lived in poor housing and often suffered bad treatment—like all prostitutes at the low end of the status hierarchy.

During the last decades of the nineteenth century, citizen groups organized to combat the traffic in Chinese women. In the 1890s prostitutes and slaves were actively rescued from those who held them. Given the option to return to China or remain in the United States, about half chose to stay. Some of these women married immigrant Chinese men, who were forbidden by U.S. law to marry Euro- or Anglo-American women (Wegars 1993:234–236).

A Comparative Analysis of Western Saloon and Brothel Sites

Alcohol and prostitution were fast partners in the West. The saloon of the mining town of the West functioned as the poor man's club (Spude 2005:90; 2015:16, citing Kingsdale 1973): the place for drinking, socializing, and keeping in touch with the news of the day. Western venues for prostitution came in several forms: tiny cribs, rooms above saloons, and parlor houses. Saloons and brothels offered alcohol and sex for cash. Simmons lacked archaeological data to test her brothel model, but Catherine Holder Spude uses material-culture data to demonstrate the similarity of saloons and brothels in the archaeological record. She also was able to discriminate between saloons and brothels.

Spude examined archaeological collections from five saloon sites and three brothel sites in western North America using functional analysis, as described in chapters 2 and 3. She selected gender-specific artifacts to develop a method to identify saloons and brothels when written documentation is lacking. The saloon collections were from Skagway and Fairbanks, Alaska; and Lake City, Colorado. Brothel collections were from Ouray, Colorado; Blairmore, Alberta; and Los Angeles, California (the only site of the eight not in a mining town). High frequencies of female-specific articles and pharmaceutical containers were associated with brothels; high frequencies of male-specific items and artifacts associated with male-dominated tasks reflected the activities of the saloon (Spude 2005:100).

Spude created an archaeological typology that selected for gender-related variables including objects used only by women and those used only by men (2005:93). Female-specific objects included clothing parts of female attire, hairpins, jewelry, cosmetic containers, sewing tools, and feminine hygiene equipment (such as douching paraphernalia). Male-specific objects included pocketknives, suspender buckles and buttons, watch fobs and pocket watches, collar stays, and razors. Personal objects such as coins, keys, and buttons not specific to men's or to women's clothing were grouped together. Artifacts with ambiguous gender associations included tobacco pipes and paraphernalia, armaments, and sewing tools (used by men in military and prison contexts) (Bush 2009:165; Spude 2005:94). Bottles that contained alcoholic beverages were separated from those containing other beverages, food, or medicine. Women often consumed alcohol in medicinal products intended for pain relief. Common cures included Lydia Pinkham's Vegetable Compound, with an alcohol content of 20.6%. Mrs. Winslow's Soothing Syrup, another favorite, included morphia. These popular pain medications were available by mail, and similar compounds could be acquired from a local pharmacy (Spude 2005:94; see also Haller and Haller 1974; Hodgson 2001).

To test the similarity of the function of saloons and brothels, Spude looked at relative frequencies of each artifact category for each saloon and each brothel collection (Spude 2005:96, Table 2; 97, Table 3) and averaged each artifact category for all saloons and all brothels. She compared the frequencies with a linear regression and found that the two datasets showed a correlation value of 0.7821, indicating high correlation (1.000 is a perfect correlation) (Spude 2005 96–97, citing Kohler and Blinman 1985; Blee 1991).

Spude compared the saloon and brothel collections with collections from four drinking family households, 10 temperate family households, 10 transient-male residences, and one priest's residence. Frequencies of the artifact categories for all six types of households demonstrate the utility of the artifact categories in isolating gender-specific artifacts (2005:95, Table 1). The analysis shows higher frequencies of alcohol-related objects, bottle closures, and male-specific objects in saloons, but high frequencies of household objects, pharmaceuticals, generic personal, and female-specific categories in brothels (Spude 2005:96, Figure 2).

In her review of the differences between the saloon collections and brothel collections, Spude notes that liquor-related objects make up a higher frequency of the collection in the saloons than in the brothels—documenting the dominance of drinking in the saloons, but not reflecting gender (2005:98). Household objects are more frequent in the brothels—reflecting the function of brothel as residence as well as workplace. In the saloon sites in the collections, only male proprietors resided in the building. Some meals were served in saloons, but clearly more meals were consumed in the brothels. Household items might be gender related, as higher percentages of household items appear in the family households, but lower percentages in the transient-male collection. However, the collection from the household occupied solely by a priest had a high frequency of household items, leading Spude to conclude that some other factor (such as length of residence) may have been involved (2005:96).

Female-specific items were more numerous in the brothel collections, and the male-specific items were more numerous in the saloons. In fact, the only male-specific items in brothel collections were two razors, two cufflinks, and a jeans rivet. Tobacco-related items accounted for nearly the same percentage in the saloons and in the brothels. In the family-household collections, however, frequencies of tobacco-related items were low, but higher in the transient-male and priest collections. Spude suggests that the presence of female family members curtailed tobacco use in family households (2005:99). Generic personal items make up a higher percentage of the brothel collections than other collections. Common activities in the brothels probably explain the frequency of buttons and coins, items easily lost during undressing and dressing (Spude 2005:99).

Brothel collections included about twice as many pharmaceutical items as the saloons. Prostitutes were constantly exposed to an array of communicable diseases and used alcohol, morphine, opium, and other drugs to treat pain. The use of pharmaceuticals may reflect both occupation and gender, as family households included more pharmaceuticals than male-only households. The differences in the percentages of pharmaceuticals between saloons and brothels, in fact, are important in discriminating between saloon and brothel middens (Spude 2005:103). Spude argues for the necessity of recognizing brothels in short-term mining camps and towns, places many had assumed were occupied overwhelmingly by men (Spude 2005:103). Just as Simmons (1989) concluded from her documentary study, Spude's archaeological analysis documented that women were an important part of the communities of the Gold Rush West. Even in the early years, women profited from the mining business and were themselves business owners and thus players in the history of the West.

Sandpoint, Idaho

Major archaeological excavations in the first decades of the twenty-first century at Sandpoint, Idaho, dramatically changed the lack-of-data problem for the mining West. Two houses of prostitution were excavated as part of the Sandpoint Archaeology Project, which began in 2006 and culminated with the release of a four-volume report in 2014. The excavations recovered more than 500,000 artifacts from several types of contexts, including shops, worker housing, a hotel, a dance hall, saloons, and brothels (Figure 4.2).

During the early twentieth century, Sandpoint changed from a frontier town, where the Restricted District (as the local red-light district was known) was quietly accepted as a popular resort, to an established and more diversified town, in which the district was no longer tolerated. It was finally closed in 1913 (Warner et al. 2014:46). The social purity movement succeeded in criminalizing vice in the early twentieth century, and red-light districts were closed throughout the country. Prostitution, of course, was not eradicated: it moved out of sight.

Two establishments documented as brothels were excavated in Sandpoint:

Figure 4.2. Historical photograph of the Restricted District, Sandpoint, Idaho. Courtesy of the Bonner County Historical Society.

Marie Henderson's brothel, occupied by Henderson, 10 women, and one male; and Willa Herman's bordello, occupied by Herman, four women, and a Chinese male. No occupant in either house is listed as a prostitute in the 1910 federal census, but other sources indicate that these households functioned as brothels. Most of the women were in their twenties; some are listed as divorced or married and with one child or more. Each house included a resident male who was listed as working in a dance hall (Warner and Bard 2014:91).

Both houses were within Sandpoint's Restricted District, near the saloon or dance hall shown in the 1909 Sanborn map. Henderson's brothel is labeled "F. B. Crib," and Herman's bordello is labeled "F. B.," for female boarding, widely used on Sanborn maps at the turn of the century to indicate a house of prostitution (Seifert 1991:89; Simmons 1989:57; Wegars 1989:25). The material culture reflects the differences between the businesses—even though they were next door to each other (Warner and Bard 2014:92, Figure 43).

Marie Henderson was the 30-year-old madam of a house that included 10 women between 18 and 30 years old. The sole male resident, 53, worked as a dance-hall musician (Warner and Bard 2014:91, citing the 1910 census). The 1909 Sanborn map and the local newspaper refer to the house as "cribs," even though the building was not the sort usually meant by the term "crib," that is, a tiny room with little more than a bed (Warner and Bard 2014:90, 92–93). Space in Henderson's brothel may have been tight, but some amenities and social activities were available to clients. For example, the archaeological record demonstrated that wine and champagne were consumed, as well as whiskey, gin, and beer. In the East, champagne was not served in houses patronized by working-class laborers. In early twentieth-century Sandpoint, however, champagne was available in both Henderson's and Herman's houses (Petrich-Guy et al. 2014:63–64; see also Warner and Bard [2014:93–94], referencing photo of Denver parlor house from Colorado Historical Society collection [Mazzulla Collection, Box 22, FF 1294, scan #10027277]). Drinking glasses also suggest a touch of class: tumblers, stemware, shot glasses, cordial glasses, and pilsner glasses were recovered from the features associated with Henderson's house.

Warner and Bard interpret the whiteware and ironstone tablewares and food-preparation vessels excavated at Henderson's brothel as ceramics used for the residents' private dining—not for entertaining clients (2014:94–95). Beef was the most common meat. Both inexpensive cuts, used for soups and stews, and expensive, individual cuts (steaks) were identified in the faunal assemblage. Warner and Bard suggest that the residents usually ate simple meals when dining alone. Expensive cuts may have been special extravagances—or occasional single-portion meals served to clients.

Willa Herman's house, the smaller establishment next to Henderson's, offered more services—not just drinking and sex—to small-business owners and managers from the local Humbird Lumber Mill. The material culture of Herman's house reflects the higher class of both patrons and residents. The artifacts reveal attention to the women's presentation: hairpins and combs, makeup, jewelry, and stack-heeled shoes (Warner and Bard 2014:96). Household objects and decorations, such as a dozen ceramic figurines, reflect household decor typical of late Victorian parlors. Herman's house offered clients drinks (wine, champagne, beer, and liquor) and hearty meals (Warner and Bard 2014:97).

Doll parts and marbles were recovered from Henderson's brothel and

Herman's bordello, suggesting that children were residing or spending time in both houses (Swords and Kisling 2014:99–100). A cap gun and lead locomotive were found in Henderson's brothel, as well as a baby tooth—lost from a child between 7.5 and 12.5 years old—although no children were listed as residents in the manuscript census (Swords and Kisling 2014:103).

Alcohol consumption was clearly an important part of the business for Henderson's brothel and Herman's bordello. In fact, the brothel and bordello contexts yielded far more alcohol bottles than saloon and hotel archaeological contexts in Sandpoint (Petrich-Guy et al. 2014:55, Table 8). Herman's bordello contexts yielded over a thousand alcohol-related tableware vessels (glasses, stemware, and tankards), far more than any other context—including Henderson's brothel (Petrich-Guy et al. 2014:55, Table 9). Wine, champagne, beer, and liquor bottles document drinking in both houses, but the differences in the clientele and class of each house are reflected in the types of alcohol consumed. The smaller, classier bordello, Herman's, yielded almost three times as many bottles (77 compared to 23). Forty-one of the bottles from her bordello, however, were Gordon's London Dry Gin. Wine and champagne were also popular choices (Petrich-Guy et al. 2014:60–61, Table 11).

Beer bottles accounted for a small percentage (3 to 4%) of the brothel and bordello alcohol-bottle assemblages, yet nine breweries were represented, including breweries in Illinois, New York, Washington, and Wisconsin. The assemblage from Sandpoint's Pend d'Oreille Hotel (163 bottles) included only four breweries. The variety of beers was yet another status marker of these establishments (Petrich-Guy et al. 2014:62).

Bitters bottles were also found in the brothel assemblages—but rarely elsewhere in Sandpoint. Bitters have an alcohol content of 30 to 40% and served several uses: as a fever treatment, an aperitif, and even an alternative to absinthe (Petrich-Guy et al. 2014:62). Three fragmentary absinthe bottles were identified in the Restricted District: two bottles of French manufacture, Pernod Fils (one each from Herman and Henderson), and one manufactured by the Swiss company Edouard Pernod (this bottle from Henderson's brothel). Absinthe includes a derivative of the wormwood plant, mixed with alcohol, anise, and herbs. It was considered a bitter aperitif, sometimes thought to have medicinal or psychotropic effects (Petrich-Guy 2014:72).

The brothel and bordello material culture also documented the special requirements of playing the part of the temporary lover. The Victorian ethos held that internal virtue, modesty, and innocence produced external ideals of feminine beauty (Kisling and Warner 2014:260, citing Peiss 1998:25). Sometimes beauty did not come naturally from internal virtues; thus, women turned to homemade or commercial products to realize the ideal. However, the painted face was thought to betray immorality and mark the prostitute (Kisling and Warner 2014:260, citing Peiss 1998:27). Thus, makeup functioned as an advertisement. Evidence of these practices in Sandpoint's Restricted District came in the form of the many grooming artifacts—many more than the number recovered from commercial and residential parts of town (Kisling and Warner 2014:260).

Herman's Bordello yielded a large assemblage of grooming and toiletry artifacts (163 items)—larger than Henderson's higher-occupancy brothel (which yielded just 83 items) and larger than any other assemblage in Sandpoint. About one-third of the items from Herman's house were containers for creams, lotions, and other skin-care products (Kisling and Warner 2014:261).

Skin whiteners included Madam Yale's Almond Blossom Complexion Cream, which claimed to clean, refine, nourish, and whiten skin. About half of the skin-care products from both bordello and brothel assemblages were intended to whiten skin or remove redness or suntan (Kisling and Warner 2014:262), suggesting pale skin was believed to make a woman desirable. Other skin-care products promised to maintain or restore a youthful complexion, such as Pompeian Massage Cream and Wakelee's Camelline. Hair-care products that promised youthful color and condition included C. Damschinsky Liquid Hair Dye, La Goutte-a-Goutte, Mrs. Potter's Walnut Juice Hair Stain, Parker's Hair Balsam, Walnut Oil, and Walnutta (Kisling and Warner 2014:263). Signs of age reduced the earning potential of a prostitute; thus, the use of products to promote youthful appearance was likely seen as an investment. Evidence of adding color to the face was found in rouge compacts made by the Elizabeth Post cosmetic company and Richard Hudnut's Three Flowers scented face powder and rouge. Colognes and perfumes included Hoyt's German Cologne (Lowell, Massachusetts), Guerlain (Paris), Dabrook's Perfumes (Detroit), and Florida Water (New York). A product made by Roger & Gallett, Paris, was found at Herman's house (Kisling and Warner 2014:264–265). Greater variety and more products were recovered from Herman's house (Kisling and Warner 2014:266).

Presenting a picture of beauty was surely an occupational requirement, especially for the women of Herman's house. Avoiding pregnancy and illness was essential. For prostitutes, pregnancy and childbirth impaired earning potential: no one visits a late-term pregnant or laboring prostitute. Access to contraception was limited, and most forms known in the late nineteenth and early twentieth centuries were illegal. From the archaeology, however, it is clear that the Sandpoint prostitutes used the methods available to them (Warner et al. 2014:31).

Numerous whole and partial vaginal and anal irrigators were recovered from Herman's bordello (Warner et al. 2014:32). Rubber tubing, a rubber bag, and hose clips of the types used with the irrigators were also recovered. All these parts are similar to those shown in contemporary advertisements for fountain syringes (also known as douche bags) (Warner et al. 2014:32). All but one of these artifacts were recovered from Herman's bordello, and none was found outside of the Restricted District. Douching was the most accessible and common form of contraception for women in the late nineteenth and early twentieth centuries. The notable advantage of douching was that it was completely under the woman's control. Use of a condom required a willing partner—perhaps not so likely with one paying for sexual services. The authors argue convincingly that the mix of vaginal and anal irrigators represents a way to circumvent the terms of the Comstock Act of 1873, which defined contraceptive devices as obscene and therefore illegal to send through the mail. Thus, douching equipment was marketed for use in maintaining family health and hygiene—sold in kits with several types of irrigators for vaginal and anal use (Warner et al. 2014:34). The women of Herman's bordello bought the whole package of family hygiene products—which could be legally sold and mailed—and selected the vaginal irrigators for postcoital douching and disposed of the other types.

These syringe kits cost just under $1.00—about the same price as a tea-kettle, man's shirt, or lady's hat (Warner et al. 2014:35). Buying a whole kit and disposing of several unwanted parts sheds light on the value of the product to a prostitute working in Herman's bordello and on her ability to afford such a purchase. Evidence of douching at Herman's bordello may also reflect the slower pace of the services offered. The women working at Herman's may have also had more time between clients, including time to take the precaution of douching to reduce the risks of pregnancy and venereal disease (Warner et al. 2014:36).

Bottles for Listerine and Vaseline were found in Restricted District contexts. Listerine was probably used as a spermicide. Vaseline (with or without boric acid) was probably also used as a barrier method of contraception—an explanation that accounts for the 22 Vaseline bottles from the Restricted District, as compared to the 4 bottles found in other contexts in town (Warner et al. 2014:36–37).

The residents of the Restricted District were constantly facing common ailments, not just venereal disease and conception. It is not surprising that twice as many patented medicines were recovered in the Restricted District as in the residential and commercial area. Only one-third of the patent medicines from the district contained alcohol or mind-altering drugs. The medicines from the rest of the town, however, were more likely to contain alcohol or opiates. Poisons were also recovered—almost exclusively—from the Restricted District. These may have been combined with other substances for contraception, rather than a means of suicide (Bard and Weaver 2014:132–133).

Venereal disease was a health risk for both prostitutes and their clients, and prostitution was thought to be the primary vector of transmission (Warner et al. 2014:38, citing Connelly 1984). Evidence of several products marketed to cure venereal disease was found in the Restricted District, all in association with Herman's bordello. Five products were remedies explicitly intended to treat venereal disease, and one was for "the unnatural discharges of men" and "debilitating weakness peculiar to women" (Warner et al. 2014:40, citing *Pend d'Oreille News* 1892:3). The authors argue that the residents of both Herman's and Henderson's houses knew how to obtain such products—and had the need for them.

Several recovered products were marketed for treating males, such as a urethral syringe designed for men. This type of syringe, found in the Restricted District, was designed to inject fluid, such as silver nitrate, boric acid, carbolic acid, and mercury compounds, into the male urethra (Warner et al. 2014:42, 44). The presence of such syringes only in the Restricted District suggests that men were seeking treatment in brothels (Warner et al. 2014:43). Warner and Bard argue that men chose to be treated for venereal diseases in brothels to avoid the cost or embarrassment of seeking medical services from a physician (2014:100).

Clients may have also sought treatment for impotence in the Restricted District. In the late nineteenth and early twentieth centuries, impotence was thought to be a consequence of excessive sexual activity. Perhaps this is why medical treatments appear malicious and even punitive. Common medical treatments included injecting caustic or blistering agents into the urethra. Thus, patent medicines that promised results without the pain were attractive and were aggressively advertised by producers. Four bottles that held solutions purported to treat impotence were recovered at Sandpoint—three from residential or commercial areas, only one from the Restricted District (Warner et al. 2014:45–46).

The hazards of visiting a brothel also included robbery, as reported in local newspapers. There were also numerous reports of "losing" wedding bands: four gold or gold-plated men's bands were recovered in the excavations of Herman's bordello. These were the only bands recovered in the excavations, and each was found within 18 feet of the others, suggesting that they were collected and cached (Warner and Bard 2014:99). Lapel pins and watch fobs— lost, strayed, or stolen—were also recovered.

The abundance and variety of artifacts recovered from Herman's bordello contrast with the assemblage from Henderson's brothel. The difference appears to reflect the targeted clientele: working-class laborers for Henderson's and middle-class business owners and managers for Herman's.

Prescott, Arizona

Several smaller-scale projects have provided data and analyses that complement the Sandpoint study and enhance our understanding of nineteenth-century prostitution in western North America. One of these projects involved the reevaluation of collections from a late nineteenth-century brothel context in Prescott, Arizona, excavated as part of a project in Prescott's city center (Foster et al. 2004). The town of Prescott was settled after gold was found in 1863. Early in the town's history, a brothel was established in Block 13, at the west edge of Prescott's original town site (Vermeer 2006:219). As the town expanded to the west, the original edge of town became the center of town; by the late nineteenth century, Block 13 was in the town center, just a block from the county courthouse (Vermeer 2006:222). Historical research indicated that Block 13 was in an informal red-light district, occupied by prostitutes and by Chinese immigrants.

Only one dense artifact concentration in Block 13 could be confidently associated with prostitution: Lot 7, the site of a brothel run by Mary Hamilton. The 1880 census lists Hamilton (40), keeping house; Mollie Martin, head; five women, prostitutes; and two children. Most of these women had one parent born in western Europe (Vermeer 2006:231–232).

Andrea Vermeer reexamined the Lot 7 artifacts, as well as the artifacts recovered from a feature in Lot 9 of Block 13, identified as the basement of a Chinese-owned building (Vermeer 2006, citing Foster et al. 2004). The house at 58/59 Granite Street, next to Hamilton's house, was occupied by a Chinese family and a prostitute (Vermeer 2006:236).

Vermeer's research approach was to develop a series of questions, hypotheses, and testing strategies and to define the material culture needed to test her hypotheses. The available data from the Prescott investigations limited her testing options; nevertheless, she offers some useful results.

Vermeer focused on the relationship between Victorian ideals and material culture from the brothel and the Chinese household. The ceramics recovered from Hamilton's brothel context appear to reflect Victorian material culture; however, the alcohol bottles and drinking glasses looked more like working-class or immigrant consumption patterns (Vermeer 2006:252). The brothel assemblage also included artifacts related to grooming—perfume, creams, high-fashion clothing—and hygiene.

The assemblage from the neighboring house at 58–59 Granite strongly reflected the documented Chinese occupation: most artifacts were manufactured in China (Vermeer 2006:253). The high financial returns of prostitution in the Chinese community are suggested by the cost of the imported Chinese ceramics and expensive meat cuts (Vermeer 2006:254). This assemblage, however, included few grooming and hygiene items.

Both Hamilton's house and the Chinese-owned house were in an informal (that is, not legally defined) red-light district, and neither household reflects a Victorian identity (Vermeer 2006:257). The material culture of Hamilton's house documented attention to grooming and hygiene (as seen in Herman's Sandpoint bordello). The occupants of the neighboring house at 58–59 Granite used few grooming products, which Vermeer suggests documents differences in production of sexuality between the two houses (2006:260).

Vermeer devotes considerable attention to placing the mining frontier in the capitalist world economy and as the site of the sudden and intense collision of cultures (2006:282). She considers women's labor in this economy, looks at how the sexual division of labor supports capitalism, and asks whether such labor is exploitive or empowering (2006:283). In the mining West, however, one can see that prostitution was a form of informal labor; in the mix of peoples and cultures in the frontier, Victorian ideology was not embraced. The economic instability of the mining community and scarcity of wage work for women would have fostered an environment where the informal labor of prostitution was one of few options open to women (Vermeer 2006:285). Prostitutes, however, contributed to formal labor by supporting entertainment enterprises (saloons and dance halls), as well as the local businesses they patronized. They also contributed to the local economy through the payment of fees and fines. Furthermore, the frontier-town brothel helped to keep money earned through mining and prostitution in the local economy. Vermeer sees prostitutes in the mining West as working women whose labor supported themselves and supported the labor of others. These women, she says, participated in the expansion of the world system and contributed to the formation, development, stability, and identity of the West (Vermeer 2006:289).

Ouray, Colorado

Mary Van Buren and Kristin A. Gensmer also reexamined archaeological collections from brothel contexts. Archaeological investigations in Ouray, Colorado, were initiated in 1970 when Steven Baker learned that the buildings on the Vanoli Block were slated for demolition (1972). Baker excavated on the block between 1972 and 1983, as the buildings were razed. Some of the artifacts were analyzed by Catherine Spude for her comparative studies of brothels and saloons (see Blee 1991; Spude 2005, discussed above). About 40 years after the excavations, students and faculty members of the Department of Anthropology at Colorado State University began recording, analyzing, and preparing the collection for curation (Van Buren and Gensmer 2017:226).

The crib girls of Ouray worked at the low end of the hierarchy of prostitution. These women rented single rooms, often for a short time before moving on to another mining town. Crib girls are rarely known to history by name. Even when they are mentioned in newspapers or documents, their names are often assumed. Van Buren and Gensmer consider how these anonymous women manipulated their appearance as workers in the sex trade (2017:219). Clothing is a way material culture is used to construct identity, and the dress of prostitutes and their clients reveals how class, gender, and work were negotiated in the Ouray red-light district (Van Buren and Gensmer 2017:19).

Van Buren and Gensmer use performance and practice theory (not consumer choice, as many early studies did) to understand the lives of prostitutes and their purchases and to focus on how women became prostitutes through the performance of their work. The prostitute's work involved creating the illusion of a relationship that was more than the exchange of sexual services for money. As has been noted elsewhere, prostitution was partly a theatrical performance by the prostitute for the client. Thus, performance theory facilitates analysis of routines that vary from social norms and allows for adoption of roles (Van Buren and Gensmer 2017:220).

Ouray, Colorado, developed from a mining camp to a town of 400 residents in the late 1870s, after silver was found in the surrounding San Juan Mountains. By 1885 the town had a population just over 1,000, mostly men between 20 and 40 years old who worked as miners (Van Buren and Gensmer 2017:221). Ouray continued to prosper after the repeal of the Sherman Silver Purchase Act in 1893, owing to the discovery of gold near the town in the late 1880s and 1890s. Industrialization of mining by the turn of the century resulted in independent miners becoming wage laborers as capitalized mining corporations dominated the industry (Van Buren and Gensmer 2017:222).

The Ouray red-light district developed along with industrialization of the mining industry. Neither the first census in 1880 nor the first Sanborn map (also 1880) shows brothels, but by 1890 the Sanborn map shows buildings marked "F. B." for female boarding (Van Buren and Gensmer 2017:223). The Vanoli Block included a six-lot sporting complex, with a saloon, a restaurant, a theater, a Chinese laundry (that functioned for a time as an opium den), and rows of cribs (Figure 4.3). In addition to the cribs, upper rooms of the saloon and theater were used by prostitutes (Van Buren and Gensmer 2017:223–224).

The complex was patronized by working-class men employed in mining or in associated work. There is little documentation on how the business of prostitution was organized in Ouray, though it seems likely that women moved often, to escape authorities or to follow demand (Van Buren and Gensmer 2017:225). Census records list women in their mid-twenties to early thirties. Most were single, widowed, or divorced; native born; and without children. These women were rarely enumerated in Ouray for more than one census. Individual women cannot be linked to specific artifacts, but the aggregation of artifacts and residents sheds light on the lives of these women (Van Buren and Gensmer 2017:226).

The analyses of artifacts from the Vanoli Block focused on excavated assemblages from yard areas between a theater and a bar known as the 220. The sample omitted assemblages that were associated with the Chinese laundry, the saloon, and rooms that may have been occupied by men working in

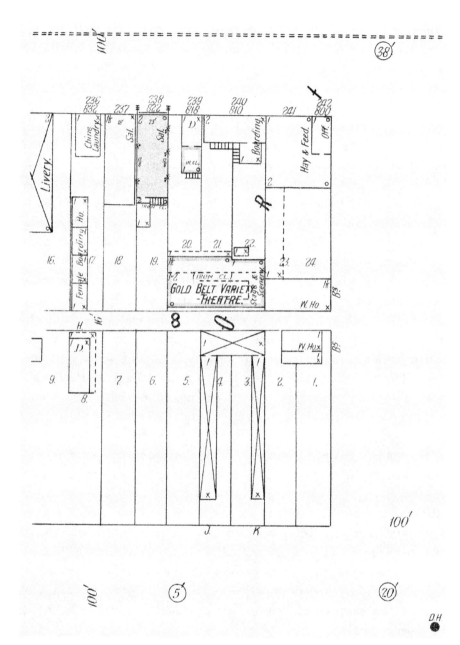

Figure 4.3. Detail of the Sanborn Fire Insurance map of Ouray, Ouray County, Colorado, 1900, sheet 3. Courtesy of the University of Colorado Library, Boulder.

the laundry. Thus, the sample focused on assemblages most likely associated with prostitution. Buttons, textile fragments, footwear, and artifacts associated with hygiene and grooming were analyzed to develop a picture of the working women and their clients (Van Buren and Gensmer 2017:230–231).

Van Buren and Gensmer found that prostitutes working in cribs in a sporting complex in the mining town dressed in working-class clothing, like their clients (2017:235). Most of the women working on the Vanoli Block wore a simple, shapeless cotton wash dress in the style known as the Mother Hubbard or prairie dress (Van Buren and Gensmer 2017:234). The archaeological record lacked fancy trims, expensive fabrics, or boning; only two corset bits were found. There was evidence, however, of a tailored cotton dress and a silk petticoat, as well as cloth-covered and other shank buttons that might have been part of stylish garments. Inexpensive dress shoes with stacked heels were recovered, but the assemblage did not include the type of slippers worn by dance-hall girls in other mining towns. Evidence for grooming included face-cream containers, combs, hairpins, toothbrushes, fragrance bottles, and jewelry (Van Buren and Gensmer 2017:235). Archaeological evidence suggests that the clients wore wool trousers and jackets, felt hats, and sturdy footwear—working-men's clothing. Cartridge casings in the assemblage suggest that those who frequented cribs—clients and prostitutes—had small handguns (that used .22 cartridges).

The prostitutes of the Vanoli Block may have taken care with grooming, but the clothing was working class, as was that of their clients. Wearing a cotton wash dress on the street would have marked a woman as sexually available. Such a dress would certainly not be worn by middle-class women away from the home. The simple clothing favored by the Vanoli Block prostitutes may have been chosen not only because of its low cost. Van Buren and Gensmer suggest that clothing marked as working class may have signaled class identity that was valued at a time and place where laborers valued class identity and distinction from middle-class mine managers and owners (2017:235).

Los Angeles, California

Prostitution was not limited to mining towns, but it had its own character in the urban West. Late nineteenth-century Los Angeles included a downtown red-light district. In response to the increase in prostitution in the 1870s, the city council passed an ordinance making the keeping of, or visits to, a house of prostitution a misdemeanor—but only in designated parts of the city (Meyer et al. 2005:107, citing Los Angeles 1878:209–221). Following enactment of the ordinance in 1874, prostitution concentrated along Alameda Street, as the city council made it legal between Third and High (Ord) Streets (Meyer et al. 2005:106). By the 1890s, however, prostitution was promoted as a city attraction. In 1894 prostitution was advertised during La Fiesta de Los Angeles, and it was listed as an entertainment in the fiesta's 1897 *Souvenir Sporting Guide* (Meyer et al. 2005:109–110).

During the 1890s brothels along Alameda Street were being replaced by brick cribs, single-room places of business. The growth of crib business in Los Angeles was partly a response to the closing of cribs in San Francisco, under the administration of Mayor James Phelan. Chris Buckley, owner of most of San Francisco's houses, moved his businesses to Los Angeles, where he joined forces with local Bartolo Ballerino. Together, they controlled most of the business in the city. By the end of the century, cribs lined Alameda Street and the intersecting street, Easy Jeanette. The buildings along Easy Jeanette Street were probably built and leased by a real estate developer, George Shafer (Meyer et al. 2005:109–110).

By the early twentieth century, a reform movement was under way to remove the cribs. Names of crib property owners were listed in the newspapers, and the district attorney later filed complaints against owners. By 1904 the overt operations were closed, but the cribs were modified to pass as legitimate business, selling tobacco or claiming to be establishments of dressmakers. Shafer's cribs were ultimately demolished and replaced by warehouses. By the end of 1904, the repurposed cribs were also slated for demolition (Meyer et al. 2005:110–111). The business moved from Alameda and Easy Jeanette Streets to adjacent Aliso Street, where prostitutes worked from rooms above first-floor businesses. By 1907 these venues of prostitution were also forced out, and the buildings were used by residential, commercial, and industrial occupants (Meyer et al. 2005:112.).

Archaeological investigations at Union Station in downtown Los Angeles in 1996 revealed a part of the city's red-light district. The excavations along Aliso Street included testing the backyards of the brothels (parlor houses), as well as three other commercial properties. Testing focused on the yard areas predicted to include filled features, such as wells, trash pits, and privies (Meyer et al. 2005:113–114).

Three contiguous backyard privies were uncovered behind a parlor house at 327 Aliso Street. In 1901 the privies were filled in when the house was connected to the city sewer. More than 10,000 artifacts associated with the 1890s occupation of the parlor house were recovered (Figure 4.4). Archaeological collections from neighboring working-class residences provided contemporaneous comparative data (Meyer et al. 2005:115–116). The research team observed substantial differences between the assemblages of the parlor house and the working-class residences. Prominent differences were seen in the consumption of food and alcohol and in grooming and health.

The researchers noted marked differences in the glassware assemblages,

Figure 4.4. Artifacts recovered from privies associated with a parlor house on Aliso Street in Los Angeles, California. Courtesy of Mary Praetzellis, Anthropological Studies Center, Sonoma State University.

when comparing the parlor house and neighboring dwellings. Drinking glasses (tumblers and stemware) account for about two-thirds of the parlor house's food-vessel assemblage, but only about one-third of the dwellings' assemblages. Glassware from the house was also notable for the number of cut, pressed, etched, and hand-blown vessels, as well as vessels of colored glass. Fewer cups and mugs came from the brothel. The role of drinking in the parlor house is demonstrated by both quantity and quality of glassware (Meyer et al. 2005:116–117). However, the parlor house did not yield a substantially higher percentage of alcohol bottles, perhaps a reflection of the success of local second-hand bottle collections (Meyer et al. 2005:118).

Alcohol consumption obviously took precedence over food consumption in the parlor house. The few vessels for serving food were mostly small porcelain dishes, the type used for small portions. Faunal remains demonstrate that beef, mutton, pork, and poultry were eaten in both the parlor house and the dwellings, but more types of fish and shellfish were enjoyed in the parlor house (Meyer et al. 2005:118–119).

Artifacts associated with grooming and health were much more common in the parlor house than in the dwellings (Meyer et al. 2005:119). Perfume and cologne bottles, cream jars, tooth-powder jars, toothbrushes, hairbrushes, combs, soap dishes, pitchers, washbasins, and chamber pots all reflect the importance of physical attractiveness in the parlor house. The health hazards of life in the parlor house were also documented in medicine bottles and vials—many from local pharmacies. The syringes in the parlor-house assemblage are testimony to efforts at contraception and treatment for venereal disease. Several quart bottles for Darby's Prophylactic Fluid were also recovered. The use of Vaseline and boric acid as a contraceptive is also documented in the assemblage, as is evidence of lactation, by a breast pump (Meyer et al. 2005:119–120).

The career of Los Angeles brothel operator Tom Savage (Kooistra 2016) sheds light on the changes taking place in the brothel business in the city at the end of the nineteenth century. The rise of Savage, the son of Irish immigrants, coincided with the decline of the independent madam as the business of prostitution moved to enterprises owned and operated by men. Savage moved from San Francisco to Los Angeles in 1887 and worked his way into the male subculture of the local red-light district. He was also involved in local boxing enterprises, a core activity of male working-class culture (Kooistra 2016:1). The career of Tom Savage illustrates the relationship between red-light districts and the male subculture of the transient and working-class laborer. These districts were sometimes identified by distinctly male names, such as Guy Town in Austin, Texas; and Buck Town, in Davenport, Iowa (Kooistra 2016:2).

The integration of saloon and brothel businesses is demonstrated by Savage's enterprises: with the lease of the Bouquet Saloon, Savage acquired the use of two rooming houses that became the core of his prostitution businesses. As with the cribs along Alameda Street, Savage operated his business in rows of narrow rooms with just a window, a space for a bed, and a washbasin—not a parlor house operated by a madam (Kooistra 2016:4). Savage became one of the most prominent of the district's businessmen. With his privileged political position, Savage was able to provide work space in his rooming houses for prostitutes forced out of the Alameda Street cribs in the 1904 purge. Savage rented his houses at highly profitable rates to prostitutes until 1907 (Kooistra 2016:6). He also protected himself from direct association with prostitution by hiring managers to actually rent the rooms (Kooistra 2016:8). By the 1920s and 1930s, the independent madams who owned, operated, and profited from the business of prostitution were displaced by male businessmen (Kooistra 2016:8).

Fargo, North Dakota

The independent-madam business model persisted longer in Fargo, North Dakota, where Melvina Massey ran a successful brothel from 1890 to 1911. Massey's operation came to light through research on the land-use history of a parking lot at the Fargo City Hall and Public Library conducted by faculty and students at North Dakota State University in Fargo. Kristen Fellows and her students knew that Melvina Massey's Crystal Palace had occupied the site, and Angela Smith's museum-studies students kept finding the name Melvina Massey in arrest records and court cases. Smith documented Massey's personal and business history from primary sources (2016); Fellows used the probate inventory to create a picture of the material culture of her parlor house (2016); and Anna Munns analyzed the related court records to understand how the business of prostitution in Fargo intersected with the law (2016). This work was done with the hope of following it with controlled excavations before a new city hall was built on the site. The following discussion does not address the archaeology, but it is included here because of the success of the research and interpretations in understanding a particular businesswoman, the material culture of her place of business, and the legal context of the business in Fargo.

Fargo was founded as the Northern Pacific Railroad Bridge was built across the Red River of the North at Moorhead, Minnesota, in 1871. Railroad towns like Fargo were occupied by the workers employed in the construction of the transcontinental railroad. Wherever transient working-class men congregated, the sex trade followed. Fargo's red-light district was in the bottomland near the river known as the Hollow. Massey bought a large lot in the Hollow and built two houses (Smith 2016:4–5).

Massey was an African American, born in Virginia in the 1830s or 1840s, most likely into slavery. She had a husband and a son, Henry Massey, who remained in Virginia with her father when she moved to Fargo to open her brothel in the 1880s. She was a businesswoman in a town with few black citizens, and she effectively worked within the legal system to maintain and protect her business interests. The sale of sexual services and the sale of alcohol were illegal in Fargo. Nevertheless, the City of Fargo benefited financially from informal regulation of illicit businesses through fining practitioners of the sex trade (Munns 2016:1, 3). Massey served time in prison for illegally selling alcohol in her brothel—but not for operating the brothel. The complementary business relationships among saloons and brothels took an unusual form in Fargo. North Dakota was dry: it was illegal to sell alcohol—that is where Massey ran into trouble with the law. Minnesota was not, however, so Moorhead saloons operated "jag wagons" to transport saloon patrons to Fargo brothels (Smith 2016:5).

Massey must have navigated at the edges of Fargo society in several ways. She was a black in an overwhelmingly white community running a successful business at the edge of propriety. She was financially successful enough to establish credit at a local furniture store and to purchase luxury goods in town (Smith 2016:7). In fact, the sex trade may have been the only option open to her for financial success. Perhaps that is why she went into business so far from her father and son living in Virginia (Smith 2016:7, 8). As a young woman in Virginia, Massey probably experienced enslavement and vulnerability to sexual exploitation (through rape or use of her own body to reproduce the slave population). In Fargo, use of her own body and those of other women as an economic resource for her own benefit may have been a notch above her Virginia experience as a black woman (Smith 2016:8–9 citing Hine 1989).

Massey's first brothel in Fargo was known as the Crystal Palace. That brothel was destroyed by arson in 1892 (one of the extralegal ways of condemning a brothel), but she probably moved the business to another building until she built her bigger and better Crystal Palace in 1903. Building permits from 1899 and 1903 include a sketch of the building, which was constructed in 1903 (Fellows 2016:2).

Massey died in 1911, and the probate inventory of her property includes a room-by-room inventory, listing furnishings and other objects of value. The downstairs included two bedrooms, a front parlor, a back parlor, a dance hall, a bathroom, and a dining room/parlor. The second floor included 11 bedrooms, all of similar size. The kitchen and sleeping space and storage space appear to have been in the basement (Fellows 2016:3).

Each parlor included an expensive parlor set for comfortable seating. The front parlor had a $200 piano, and the back-parlor floor was covered by a $65 carpet. Fellows suggests that the furnishings would have created an environment comfortable to a middle- and upper-class clientele. Additional seating and two cuspidors in the back parlor suggest that it was probably used for socializing among admitted clients and the resident women, while the front parlor functioned as a reception and screening space (Fellows 2016:4).

Socializing was probably also a function of the dining room/parlor, identified in the inventory as Room #1. The inventory entry for this room included a parlor set, an iron couch cushioned with fancy pillows, and a center table, as well as glass tumblers, plates, and a punch bowl—all of which suggest a room for dining and drinking, which may well have been as important a revenue stream as sexual services (Fellows 2016:4–5, 7). Although North Dakota was a dry state, alcohol was probably available in the Crystal Palace. Remember that Massey spent time in jail for serving it (Fellows 2016:8; Smith 2016:4).

The Crystal Palace also included a dance hall on the first floor, complete with a piano, 5-by-5-foot mirror, 18 wire soda-fountain chairs, an electric chandelier, and an electric fan valued at $13.50 (Fellows 2016:5). The dance hall may have accommodated both social dancing and performances for the clients, activities frequently associated with drinking and prostitution, though not always in the same establishment (as in Skagway and Ouray). The parlor, dining, and dance spaces in the Crystal Palace demonstrate the multiple functions of the establishment. Socializing and drinking among male clients and with female working women were clearly important attractions of the Crystal Palace, as well as revenue-producing activities. The business of sex upstairs was not the sole function of Massey's establishment.

The probate inventory demonstrates that the downstairs rooms were well appointed for social intercourse. Not so the upstairs rooms, including an upper hall and 11 bedrooms, each with a chair, dresser, commode, bed frame, and mattress. Melvina Massey's first-floor bedroom had contents valued at $185.50. The upstairs bedrooms' average value was $16.50. This average value does not include personal items, as these things belonged to individual women, who would have taken their own property with them. The value of property in Massey's own room speaks to her wealth (Fellows 2016:6).

Anna Munns investigated the police magistrate court dockets from late 1893 to late 1901 (2016:4), where she found that most charges were filed against madams for keeping a house of ill fame (212) compared to charges filed against prostitutes for being an inmate of a house of ill fame (45) (Munns 2016:5). Women working independently were charged with keeping a room for the purpose of prostitution, resorting to rooms for the purpose of prostitution, or vagrancy (Munns 2016:6). Madams and inmates of high-class brothels usually paid the fine, were released, and returned to work. Women without financial resources served the time.

Men also appear in the police magistrate court documents, but not as often as women. Over the eight-year period that was examined, there were 288 charges against women and just 16 charges against men. Several of the male defendants were identified only by their first initial and last name; thus, men were permitted some measure of legal anonymity not available to women (Munns 2016:7). Some men, in fact, were discharged without serving time or paying a fine, and the fines levied against men ($10.83) were consistently lower than those paid by independent women ($14.17) (Munns 2016:8).

Madams and the inmates of their brothels were regularly arrested and fined: madams were fined a monthly rate of $31.50; each inmate, $11.50. In August of 1895 the fines were consolidated into a monthly rate of $56.50, paid by the madam for the whole house (Munns 2016:8–9). Madams apparently quietly paid the fines as a cost of doing business and thereby avoided significant disruption to the establishment. Women who did not benefit from the insulation of a brothel were fined at higher rates. Clearly, overall, women paid the price of business in the sex trade—to the benefit of the city of Fargo (Munns 2016:9–10).

The West of the Imagination and the West of Evidence

Prostitution came to the nineteenth-century West with miners, loggers, and cattle drivers and the settlements that supported their undertakings. The Euro-

American, African American, Hispanic, and Chinese laborers who came to the West to make their fortunes, or just looking for wage labor, were overwhelmingly male and single or living as single men (unaccompanied by wives or other dependent family members). The demand for female companionship and sex was high. Women who came West looking for wage labor found few opportunities other than domestic services, but sexual services were in demand and far more lucrative than conventional women's work.

The sales of alcohol and sex were complementary business enterprises in the West, as they were in the East, and both became important revenue sources for private entrepreneurs and local government. The brothels of Hooker's Division in Washington, DC, ran into trouble selling liquor without a license (as reported in a local newspaper article titled "Within Sight of the White House" [1895]), and Melvina Massey was jailed for selling liquor in dry North Dakota—not for selling sex (Smith 2016:4). The association of tangible evidence for alcohol consumption (bottles and glasses) and the more tenuous material evidence for commercial sex is important in recognizing prostitution in the archaeological record. Analyses of archaeological assemblages from western saloons and brothels by Catherine Spude and by Mark Warner and James Bard address the complexity of identifying venues of prostitution.

The degree of acceptance and integration of prostitution changed as settlements developed from mining camps and small settlements to organized towns managed by capitalized industrial enterprises or governed by elected municipal officials. The integration of wives and families prompted the segregation of sporting or vice districts, where prostitution, drinking, gambling, and opium use were concentrated, by either statute or custom. Further segregation followed racial and ethnic lines, with Chinese laborers, families, businesses, and brothels most likely to be restricted to the local Chinatown.

The case of Chinatown and Chinese prostitutes inevitably raises the question of agency. Chinese prostitutes were nearly always held in bondage—whether kidnapped, indentured, or sold to Chinese managers. Many of the young Chinese women brought to North America thought they were coming to a new husband or to wage labor. That future was rarely realized (Simmons 1989:13–14, 139; Wegars 1993:231).

The question of agency for most women in the business is complicated. It seems likely that there were women who chose to enter the business of running a brothel, such as Melvina Massey in Fargo and Ah Toy in San Francisco

(Smith 2016; Wegars 1993). Marie Henderson and Willa Herman appear to have made a success of the business in Sandpoint, whatever their motivations for embarking on the endeavor (Warner and Bard 2014). We have no first-person accounts of these women's experiences or assessments of their choices. Those accounts we have, as Catherine Spude (2005) points out, warrant critical evaluation and leave us suspecting the narrators were constructing a narrative to entertain a specific, uncritical audience.

A critical view of commercial sex leads one to consider the nature of choice for those involved in selling sex as a continuum: victims of trafficking, prostituted people, survivors, and sex workers (Steele 2017:245–246). Even sex workers—those who choose the work—may be seen making a choice to engage in commercial sex when there are no better options, a choice made by someone experiencing homelessness, poverty, lasting effects of abuse in childhood, and lack of education and job skills (Steele 2017:244). Thinking about agency as a continuum on the spectrum of choice may help us understand the experiences of women involved in commercial sex in the American West.

Andrea Vermeer gathered some statements that give voice to a broader range of thoughts of women engaged in commercial sex, which speak overtly and obliquely to agency:

Dolly Arthur: By the time I was 18 or 19 I realized I could make a lot more money from the attentions of men than I could waiting tables. . . . I was hardly ever mistreated, you know. Most men are gentlemen if you are decent with them. (Vermeer 2006:203, citing Allen 1976:12, 58)

Lillian Powers: Well, my father had this farm, you see, and nobody to work it but him and us two girls. I was fourteen, two years older than my sister, and he forgot most of the time that we wasn't horses. . . . One morning, I decided that instead of going to the field to plow, I would run away to Alton, the next town, a few miles from St. Louis. . . . I got a job in a laundry and if you think that was easy, my God! It was almost as bad as the farm and my pay was fifty cents a week. . . . I took up with the girl who worked next to me . . . and I asked her how she made out on such a piddling wage. "I don't," she said. "None of us girls do on what they pay us. Every last one of us has had to get ourselves a pimp. The quicker you do this the better off you'll be." (Vermeer 2006:204, citing Lee 1968:50–51)

Madeleine Blair: I could not make a demonstration of affection over men or any pretense or response to their caresses. For the life of me, I could not understand why they should expect it. They had only bought my body. I could not see why they should want more. My love was not for sale, piecemeal, to every man who had the price to pay for my body, and I could make no pretense at a response I did not feel. (Vermeer 2006:206, citing Blair 1986:71)

These few statements offer insight into how some of the practitioners thought about their lives. Local newspapers tell us that prostitutes were not uniformly condemned within their communities.

Sandpoint's Restricted District was separated from the rest of the business district by the railroad tracks, Sand Creek, and Bridge Street. It may have been on the wrong side of the tracks, but the occupants of the Restricted District appear to have enjoyed a level of respect as community residents. In a newspaper report of a local robbery in the Restricted District, the reporter takes issue with the accusation that Trixie Colton stole money from a lumberjack who was visiting the district. The report says that the "Colton woman has never been implicated in a robbery while she has been here, a period of six years, and the police do not believe she got the money" (Warner and Bard 2014:89 citing *Pend d'Oreille Review* 1909:1). Report authors Mark Warner and James Bard point out that the police did not believe the lumberjack's account (that Colton threw him down and took his money) and declined to believe that she was to blame for the crime (Warner and Bard 2014:89–90).

Census records do not list the name of Trixie Colton, but any woman in the Restricted District was surely working in the sex trade, and the lumberjack may have figured that his word would be trusted over hers. However, it seems likely that the police knew Colton, and they declined to believe she was a robber—even though she worked in a brothel (Warner and Bard 2014:90).

Newspaper coverage of women in Prescott suggests that prostitutes received sympathetic coverage when two were murdered during robberies in 1870, but less respect was shown in newspaper coverage for departing female missionaries and for a woman who left her husband, who was described in the paper as a soiled dove (Vermeer 2006:229–230).

The business of prostitution in the West shares several common features with the enterprise in the East. In the earliest stages of settlement in the West, prostitutes were less likely to be segregated in sporting or red-light districts, and more likely to be accepted—or even welcomed—as independent businesswomen. Research on prostitution in the East, especially research including investigation of archaeological sites, has primarily addressed nineteenth- and twentieth-century urban sites. By the second decade of the twentieth century, towns and cities across the United States were taking steps to close brothels and red-light districts and to criminalize prostitution. The business of sex did not go away, but it is harder to see in the historical and archaeological records.

5

Clandestine Pursuits

Public Defiance of the Rules

As we have already seen, clandestine pursuits are not always illegal, and they are not even always clandestine. Prostitutes, dressed to the nines, paraded on Broadway in mid-nineteenth-century New York. Everyone knew they were prostitutes; it was what they actually did that you weren't supposed to acknowledge. Prostitutes, however, hid their true identities. The clandestine parts of their lives were not their work as prostitutes, but rather, who they were when they weren't prostitutes. Women who turned to prostitution in the nineteenth century generally came from the working class (for example, see Roberts 1992; Rosen 1982). To succeed in the business, they imitated the values of their middle-class clients while laughing at "bourgeois morality" behind their backs (Roberts 1992:237). According to former factory worker and dancer Nickie Roberts, prostitution was not a disgraceful profession from a working-class perspective. It was done out of economic necessity, and it was done in the context of a culture that was "communal, raucous, anti-patriarchal," and considerably more relaxed about sex than was bourgeois culture. Prostitution, she says, was "firmly embedded in—not distinct from—the culture of the urban working classes" (1992:237). It was in no way shameful, and as has been pointed out many times, it paid considerably better wages than any other work available to working-class women in the nineteenth century.

Other kinds of clandestine activities were done for other reasons. Wage workers rebelled against authority by resisting rules and regulations and even sabotaging production. Consumers participated in illicit economic behavior, what Kathleen Deagan has called a "quintessential historical archaeological issue" (Deagan 2007:113). They defied regulations regarding what they could or could not buy; they did not restrict themselves to goods obtained legally but instead bought what they liked and could afford. Once overseas trade connected America to the rest of the world, Americans indulged their appetites for material goods, a trait that has continued into the present. People took risks to get what they wanted. Prisoners planned escapes and endured conditions not visible from the outside, and enslaved Africans escaped to freedom by constructing elaborate networks of communication, both human and physical. Privateers and pirates avoided trade regulations and, in the most dramatic cases, were robbers at sea. All of these activities left evidence behind, and to a great extent that evidence, discovered archaeologically, adds a complexity to the past that is otherwise unavailable. It reveals agency where agency wasn't always obvious and lets us see what is, at the very least, unconventional and often courageous behavior.

Resistance in the Nineteenth Century

Beginning as early as the American Revolution, resistance to power has been integral to the American experience. In the context of industrial capitalism, resistance has taken many forms, all requiring agency, both individual and collective (Saitta 2007). Conditions of exploitation, low wages, and boring and meaninglessness jobs have inspired both public and private acts of resistance. Among public acts are strikes, work slowdowns, walkouts, and intentional property damage; private ones for which there is archaeological evidence generally resulted from individual actions, from individuals' willingness to use their agency to defy the rules. Low wages and poor living and working conditions, as well as a lack of control over both, led some workers to rebel at their bosses' expense. Evidence of what were often creative and daring acts has been found by archaeologists on work sites even if the acts remained secret when they were committed.

Defiance in the Workplace

Michael Nassaney and Marjorie Abel (2000) interpreted the large quantity of discarded artifacts along the riverbank near the former cutting room and trip hammer shop of the John Russell Cutlery Company in Turners Falls, Massachusetts, as "a form of defiance against the implementation of the new industrial labor system, which closely regulated their work" (Shackel

2009:56). The John Russell Cutlery Company, which was begun in 1833 along the Green River in Greenfield, Massachusetts, relocated to a much larger facility in Turners Falls in 1870 and there became "the largest cutlery company in the world" (Nassaney and Abel 2000:242). Production methods were converted into a series of standardized, repetitive tasks, which resulted in the "near complete separation of the conception of production by managers from the execution of labor" (2000:258). As in other industries, labor was de-skilled, work was monotonous, and production was speeded up to the benefit of the managers.

Besides describing all sorts of artifacts relating to the production process—raw-material scraps, cut-out metal, cutlery wasters—discarded by the riverbank, Nassaney and Abel describe at least one discarded knife from later in the manufacturing process. An oral informant, who had worked in the factory, claimed that workers avoided admitting manufacturing mistakes by throwing objects out the window into the river. There is also the possibility that "workers may have spoiled knives intentionally—a form of industrial sabotage—as a way to regain some degree of autonomy on the shop floor" (2000:268).

Paul Shackel has described how workers "drank the owners' profits while they operated machinery" at the Harpers Ferry Brewery in the late nineteenth and early twentieth centuries (Shackel 2000:236). More than a hundred beer bottles were found between the walls of the bottling works, and more than a thousand were found down the building's elevator shafts during the renovation of the beer bottling works in 1995 and 1996. The bottles dated between 1893 and 1909, a period when workdays averaged between 14 and 18 hours six days a week, and 6 to 8 hours on Sundays. Shackel speculates that the workers drank on the job and concealed their subversive behavior by disposing of the bottles out of the view of supervisors.

Evidence of drinking on the job was also found on the site of a major repair facility at the Lakehurst repair shops for the Raritan and Delaware Bay (later the Central) Railroad in New Jersey. Archaeologists Richard Veit and Paul Schopp reported finding several large caches of liquor bottles dating from the late nineteenth and early twentieth centuries in concealed places, even though most railroads had established regulations against drinking by the 1850s (Veit and Schopp 1999:21). Employment in the Raritan and Delaware rail shops was consistent between 1900 and 1912, but when the main shop for the railroad, located elsewhere, was expanded, the number of workers at Lakehurst dropped

from about 105 men to about 75. Veit and Schopp speculate that workers about
to lose their jobs in a railroad town may not have paid much attention to rules
against drinking.

The bottles were found in service pits below the stalls of the roundhouse, in
a small rectangular space located at the north end of the last roundhouse stall,
and in the flywheel pit of the stationary engine room. The service pits at Lakehurst allowed workmen access to the undersides of locomotives, particularly
the running gear. Out of a total of 1,107 artifacts recovered from these pits, 556
were bottles or fragments of bottles. Of the 103 bottles that could be identified,
71 were flasks, the kind that could be easily carried in a workman's pocket and
would likely contain alcohol (Figure 5.1). Most of the flasks were manufactured in automated molds or semi-automated molds, thus dating them after
1903. Another 31 flasks dating to the early twentieth century were found in the
flywheel pit. Out of a total of 326 artifacts found in a shallow deposit near the
roundhouse, 311 of them belonged to bottles. Of the 48 bottles identified, 46

Figure 5.1. Flasks from excavations of the Lakehurst repair shops, Raritan and Delaware Bay
Railroad. Courtesy of Richard Veit, Monmouth University.

were half-pint flasks manufactured between 1870 and 1890, suggesting that even before their jobs were threatened, there was a tradition of drinking on the job. Veit and Schopp (1999:37) argue that "on the job drinking was a form of workplace resistance to the impersonal forces of the capitalist economy." Working conditions were uncomfortable, especially when plans were being made to phase out the facility.

Worksites are not the only place evidence of illicit drinking has been recovered. Liquor bottles were found where they shouldn't have been in the Lowell Boardinghouse backlots at the Boott Mills industrial complex in Massachusetts. The Boott Mills complex, a National Park Service site that was excavated in the mid-1980s (e.g., Beaudry 1989, 1992; Mrozowski et al. 1996), employed mostly young, unmarried, Irish immigrant women who were strictly forbidden from a long list of things, including reading, singing, drinking, meetings, leaving work, and gambling. The presence of alcohol bottles was a surprise to the archaeologists, who did not think boardinghouse rules would be disobeyed. Evidence of drinking included bottles for liquor, wine, and beer, as well as beer mugs and wine glasses. Kathleen Bond, who studied the Lowell evidence of alcohol consumption for her master's thesis, thought "it was impossible to tell from the archaeological data whether drinking promoted working class solidarity or was rooted in ethnic traditions and a pre-industrial work ethic" (Beaudry 1992:93, quoting Bond 1989).

Besides drinking among the workers, the presence of bottles in archaeological deposits at Lowell revealed something about the bosses. The largest number of alcohol bottles came from two privies that the Board of Health had ordered closed in 1890. The 700 machine-made bottle fragments recovered indicated that the privies could not have been filled until after 1910, when those kinds of bottles were available. Besides evidence of illicit drinking, the artifacts provided incontrovertible evidence that the paternalistic Lowell Mills Corporation did not obey Board of Health instructions. The archaeological evidence, plus interviews with a former boardinghouse resident, indicates that the privies were probably still in use more than twenty years after they were supposed to be closed.

Agency under Wraps

Perhaps even more surprising than the archaeological evidence for resistance to nineteenth-century working conditions is the evidence of resistance found on prison sites. Among the architectural gems in Philadelphia is Eastern State Penitentiary, designed by John Haviland in 1829 (Figure 5.2). Amazingly enough, the prison, with its forbidding facade, gothic turrets, 30-foot-high walls, and huge metal gate, was still in use in the 1960s. It was almost demolished in the 1980s, but an effort by preservationists managed to save the structure. Since the 1990s the public has been able to visit its crumbling cells. Haviland's design conformed to a radial style that was being used in Britain at the time. Seven cell blocks radiate out from a central hub, which supposedly promoted "watching, convenience, economy, and ventilation." Each cell has its own exercise yard, flush toilet, and source of heat and ventilation. Isolation in combination with religious contemplation was intended to inspire rehabilitation, the Quaker penal philosophy at the time. Although prisoners were eventually allowed to exercise together, communication among them was always discouraged. It was only in its later years that inmates shared cells.

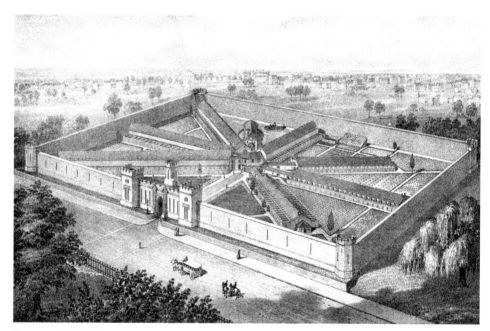

Figure 5.2. *Eastern State Penitentiary.* Drawing by Samuel Cowperthwaite, convict number 2954. Reproduced in Johnston 1994:199.

Haviland's radial design put the cells on the end of each spoke close to the prison yard, and a prisoner named Clarence Klinedinst took advantage of the yard's proximity to dig an escape tunnel in the 1940s. Klinedinst was a mason by trade, and while doing plastering for the prison, he managed to leave an opening in a cell wall, which he camouflaged with a removable panel. Claiming the cell as his own, he began digging the tunnel at night, first alone and then with a cellmate. The finished tunnel extended across the yard for 97 feet and dipped down to 15 feet to get under the outside wall. It had electricity cleverly hooked up to an outlet in Klinedinst's cell and was shored with wooden scraps, probably stolen from prison workshops. On the morning of April 3, 1945, Klinedinst, his cellmate, William Russell, and 10 other men, including famous bank robber Willie Sutton, crawled through the tunnel to a short-lived freedom. Sutton was apprehended almost immediately, Klinedinst in a few hours, and most of the others within a few days. Only one of the escapees remained at large; another came to the door of the prison and asked to be re-admitted. It was too cold outside (Johnston 1994).

While Sally Elk, the executive director of what is now the Eastern State Penitentiary National Historic Landmark, and her staff knew about the tunnel and the details of its construction from the transcribed interviews with escapees after they were apprehended, they didn't know its exact alignment and whether it was still open, aspects of the tunnel that visitors always asked about. As part of the sixtieth anniversary celebration of the prison escape, they hired John Milner Associates (JMA) to use archaeology to address these questions.

It was easy to find the exit to the tunnel, since there were photographs of prison authorities examining the escape hole outside the wall, but exposing the entry was a challenge. After the escape, prison personnel filled up the entry to the tunnel in Klinedinst's cell with concrete, and even two days with a jackhammer reached only the very beginning of the place where the tunnel began to trend downward. JMA used ground-penetrating radar to determine the alignment of the tunnel across the yard and an augur to see whether it was still open. On a second try, the augur hit a void at about 8.5 feet below the surface that extended to about 10.5 feet. The JMA team then dropped a sewer camera (made for detecting problems in sewer pipes) down into the hole to see the tunnel interior. At first, the only thing visible was the floor of the tunnel, but manipulating the lens finally brought a glimpse of jumbled wooden shoring. This appeared to confirm that the tunnel, or at least a portion of it, was still open, but site personnel wanted to know more.

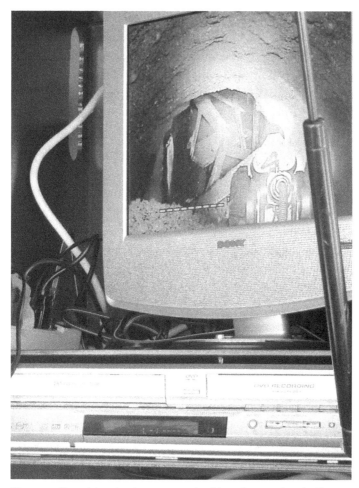

Figure 5.3. Tunnel interior image transmitted by robot crawler, April 2006. From Yamin 2008:Figure 10.17.

A year later JMA came back with a fancier camera mounted on a robotic crawler that "saw" the arch of the tunnel, shoring still in place, and an electrical wire with a split connection at the end hanging off one of the pieces of shoring (Figure 5.3). The story of the construction of the tunnel and the archaeology that confirmed its existence are still told in a video shown on site in the cell adjacent to the one where the tunnel began. Like so many clandestine (often illegal) activities, there is something irresistibly interesting about proof of ingenuity and human agency in difficult circumstances. In this case, the tunnel was secretly dug through silty clay fill deposited to level the ground before the prison was built. It is a miracle it didn't collapse during construction, and an even greater miracle that it remains open.

Tunnels like the one at Eastern State Penitentiary are still being dug, and there are probably plenty more that could be investigated archaeologically, but there are also other kinds of evidence for clandestine behavior inside penal institutions. James Garman (2005) studied the Rhode Island State Prison site in Providence using the results of extensive archaeological excavations done by the Public Archaeology Lab (PAL) in anticipation of construction of the Providence Place Mall. Also designed by John Haviland, the Rhode Island State Prison was originally built in 1838, nine years after Eastern State Penitentiary. Communal workshops were added between 1845 and 1850, and two cell block wings, a large workshop, and a boiler house were added in the 1850s. The prison's restricted site, however, prevented it from ever reaching a size adequate to accommodate the growing population of inmates, and by 1878 it was abandoned for a newly built facility outside the city.

Haviland did not attempt the radial design he had used in Philadelphia but instead designed a linear building consisting of a keeper's house in the front, a connecting building behind it, and the cellblock running from south to north behind that. Like Eastern State, the facility was to be enclosed in a high (14-foot) wall running 100 feet east–west by 194 feet north–south, with the keeper's house sited in the middle of the front wall. The 40 original cells were intended for individual prisoners who, according to the philosophy of the day, would benefit from solitary confinement. "The idea was to cut off the prisoner completely from any source of contamination that would engender a return to a former life of deviance" (Garman 2005:42). Inmates worked by themselves—at shoemaking in Rhode Island—in their cells and exercised in their own yards. Called the Pennsylvania Plan, it was supplanted in the mid-1840s with the Auburn Plan, which was the plan that most prisons were using by that time. In the Auburn Plan convicts still slept in individual cells, but they worked in communal workshops in the daytime and exercised in a common prison yard. Neither plan allowed convicts to talk to one another, but the Auburn Plan at least allowed some human contact.

As at Eastern State, the inmates in Rhode Island found ways to communicate in spite of the restrictions against it. On September 1, 1847, 12 inmates fled the county jail workshop while officers were at dinner. They crossed the prison yard and used a pile of lumber to scramble over a coal shed and finally over the outside wall. It is more than likely that they had communicated this plan with each other and possibly with prison personnel who directed them to the woodpile (Garman 2005:151). Eleven of the twelve were apprehended. In 1872 two more inmates, Elisha Peck and Charles Williams, apparently in cahoots, escaped from the old cellblock, Williams remaining permanently free (Garman 2005:112). Other attempted escapes involved passing coded notes to associates on the outside (that did not work) and overpowering a guard in the chapel and running for the walls. There is no archaeological evidence for these escape attempts, but other kinds of evidence point to other kinds of resistance to the power of the state. Among them were clandestine meetings between prisoners of different sexes—there were a few women in the prison from the very beginning—the stashing of contraband beneath cell floors (it is not clear whether it was found archaeologically), and the forbidden decoration of cell walls (Garman 2005:112). Prisoners occasionally refused to work in the workshops, intentionally worked slowly, destroyed tools, and spoiled prison property.

The most specific archaeological evidence for clandestine activities at Rhode Island State Prison implicates the prison authorities, rather than the inmates. The archaeological investigation of the subsoil in the east and west prison yards revealed more than 200 features, including trash pits, filled wells and cisterns, and postholes. As described by Garman (2005:108), the prison yard would have been "a filthy, muddy area marked by large trash pits of noisome material." The archaeologists found a rectangular, slate-lined feature (3 meters by 1.5 meters) built into the yard wall near a workshop that was filled with more than 10,000 pieces of animal bone, apparently waste from the manufacture of bone buttons and other implements. The pit was so foul that a slate-lined sluice had been built to drain liquid waste from the bone. There were also piles of ash, slag, and vitrified residue shoveled out of the furnace surrounding the boiler house. This fouled landscape was invisible from the outside of the prison, but the warden had "put inmates to work hauling loam, planting trees, and otherwise gentrifying the front of his house" (Garman 2005:113) to soften the forbidding starkness of Haviland's design. Nothing, however, was done to beautify, or just make bearable, the prison yards behind it, which could not be seen by the public from the outside of the building. Interestingly, Garman interprets the warden's landscaping efforts as "active subversion . . . wrought not just by the 'powerless' (inmates) but by everyone who operated inside the institutional matrix" (Garman 2005:113). The lack of landscaping to the rear is left uninterpreted.

Another archaeological find exposed prison authorities' attempts to discipline inmates. Cobblestone walks that were uncovered are not described in any documents. The walks, undoubtedly built under coercion by inmates, were two feet wide and spaced far enough apart to discourage any talking or joking among the inmates as they marched from their cells to the workshops. Perhaps the walkways achieved their intended objective, at least publicly, but the evidence for escape attempts means that prisoners found other places to talk (and plan). The archaeological investigation of the basement of the west wing revealed cells barely large enough for a man to lie down (4 by 6 feet across) and completely devoid of light. Used for solitary confinement of repeat offenders, these cells were located in the wettest part of the site. In Garman's words, "Here is institutional authority's ultimate response to unruly labor: bury it, often for days at a time, in the deepest, darkest hole imaginable" (Garman 2005:177).

Clandestine acts thus are not always about resistance to power. In fact, the material evidence from Rhode Island State Prison speaks more to acts committed by the powerful against the powerless. As Robert Paynter and Randall McGuire point out, power is heterogeneous; it "percolates through society" (1991:12). There is "power to" and "power to fail to comply" (1991:11). Both may be revealed archaeologically, and while neither is necessarily clandestine, archaeology may reveal clandestine examples that are otherwise invisible.

The Underground Railroad

The Underground Railroad refers to the network of secret routes taken by escaped slaves to freedom in the years before the Civil War. Never an actual railroad, escapees were guided from one safe house (or hiding place) to another by those known as conductors on the railroad. Quakers in Pennsylvania and elsewhere were dedicated to finding effective ways to abolish slavery, and many were active in the Underground Railroad, although they may have been given more credit than was deserved (Barbour and Frost 1988:8).

Evidence of the Underground Railroad is notoriously difficult to find for a variety of reasons. Fabled tunnels and secret hiding places often turn out not to exist or to be something else altogether. It is also true that until relatively recently, free black communities that participated in the Underground Railroad were not recognized. A recent book focusing on these communities by Cheryl LaRoche makes clear the important role they played in the Underground Railroad and the role historical archaeologists may have to play in finding them (LaRoche 2014:x). LaRoche's book identifies four small, midwestern, free black communities—Rocky Fork, Miller Grove, Lick Creek, and Poke Patch—that had not previously been recognized as stops on the Underground Railroad. Through a combination of oral history, primary documents, and the identification of distinctive landscape features, LaRoche was able to describe these communities, which in every case were near known centers of abolitionist activity, including an African Methodist Episcopal (AME) church and Underground Railroad stations. LaRoche argues for the centrality of the AME church in the Underground Railroad landscape. Founded by Richard Allen in 1816, the AME Church initiated and supported many antislavery campaigns, including the Underground Railroad (Newman 2008). The original church was in Philadelphia, but by 1846 there were 296 AME churches and nearly 20,000 congregants.

A rebuilt AME church, a few foundations, and the original terrain are all that survive of Rocky Fork, a very small settlement in Illinois that was located three miles northwest of Alton, a major Underground Railroad station and one of Illinois's main abolitionist centers. Rocky Fork was well situated as a stop on the Underground Railroad because of its accessibility to the Mississippi River via several creeks.

Two landscape features, Sand Cave and Crow Knob, plus a few foundations and cultivated plants, mark the location of Miller Grove, also in Illinois. Bonfires were apparently lit on top of Crow Knob "to guide escaping slaves toward the safety of Miller Grove," where there was an AME church and a school (LaRoche 2014:53). Although several slates have been retrieved archaeologically, the foundation of the school has not yet been located. Miller Grove's "proximity [to] the river [the Mississippi] and prospects for a railway passing through the region" were extolled in a letter written by a white abolitionist Bible salesman (LaRoche 2014:51).

A little graveyard is the only visible remnant of the Lick Creek settlement, known as "Little Africa," in southern Indiana (LaRoche 2014:57). The settlement was located 20 miles north of the Ohio River, which marks the border with Kentucky. Archaeological findings revealed that the Lick Creek settlement consisted of scattered log houses. Paul Quinn, an elder of the AME Church, built churches southwest of Lick Creek along the Ohio River, and the community was apparently part of a network of stops on the Underground Railroad that led from Kentucky north through Indiana.

Poke Patch in southern Ohio was marked distinctively in the landscape by its association with iron mines. Branches of the Underground Railroad apparently passed though stations along the southern borders of the Ohio River, while a northern route leading to Poke Patch passed through the Hanging Rock Iron Region, a 30-mile-long iron-ore belt that included four counties in Ohio and the northern portion of Kentucky. When it began in the 1820s, Poke Patch included freed African Americans, whites, mulattos, and Native Americans, all of whom were involved in assisting escapees. A wealthy white industrialist and furnace operator, John Campbell, subsidized the Underground Railroad in the area, frequently supplying horses, saddles, and wagons. According to LaRoche (2014:74), "ironmasters stood out among abolitionists who exploited their company towns, ironworks, and access to transportation routes to move runaways through the landscape, often from one furnace to another."

It is clear from LaRoche's work that the role of small black communities in the Underground Railroad has not been fully appreciated. The sites, often abandoned communities with no remaining standing structures, are invisible in the landscape unless you know where to look. LaRoche believes it may be historical archaeologists who are best suited to find and study these sites using a combination of excavation and mapping (2014:101). Such study would surely add immeasurably to an understanding of how the Underground Railroad really worked—how people moved invisibly through the landscape and who guided them.

On a much smaller scale, several archaeological investigations in the Northeast have turned up convincing evidence relating to hiding places used by escapees on the Underground Railroad. The Parvin Homestead, near Reading, Berks County, Pennsylvania, is a classic case of property owners wanting stories of Underground Railroad "tunnels" on their property to be true. According to James Delle and Jason Shellenhamer, archaeologists who investigated the Parvin site, "the Underground Railroad had a long history in Reading and surrounding Berks County" (2008:43). The most likely Parvin family member to be involved was Jacob (1815–1895), who lived in the homestead for his entire life and was a member of the Society of Friends in Reading. Jacob made changes to the eighteenth-century homestead in 1856, including the addition of a cold cellar on the front lawn.

Three openings interpreted as possible tunnels were revealed during renovations to the Parvin property made by new owners in the 1990s. One of the openings was Jacob's "new" cold cellar (there was also an older one near the kitchen at the back of the house), another was in the main house, and still another was in the barn. In keeping with Parvin family stories, the owners imagined that the "openings" were entrances to tunnels through which fugitives crawled from Willow Creek up to the house. The purpose of the archaeological investigation was to determine how the tunnels worked.

Four 2-by-2-m test units were used to look for the tunnels. Three of the four turned up nothing, but the one placed inside the new cold cellar, in front of an opening in its wall that appeared to be an alcove, suggested that it might actually have been a hiding place. The unit was extended into the stone-lined alcove, which continued into the cellar wall for a distance of almost 2 m and ended on a hard-packed dirt wall. There was no entrance to a tunnel, but according to the archaeologists, the space inside the alcove (about 2 m high and 1.5 m wide) could have accommodated one to three people in relative comfort. The opening from the root cellar proper into the alcove was just 1.3 m high by 1 m wide and would have been concealed by standing objects in front of it. The floor of the alcove was slightly higher than the floor of the cold cellar, thus preventing water on the floor of the cold cellar from entering the alcove.

While the alcove did not lead to a tunnel, the artifacts found inside suggest that escapees may have spent a substantial amount of time there. Of the 332 artifacts found, the most telling were two chamber pots, not something that is usually found in a cold cellar. Chamber pots are also something that would be needed only if people were spending a long time in seclusion. Other artifacts included sherds of various ceramic vessels for storage and eating, butchered bones (possibly the remains of meals), fragments from three medicine bottles, and a single blue, faceted, glass bead. The blue bead was considered particularly noteworthy because of the consistent association of blue beads with African American sites (Delle and Shellenhamer 2008:53). The new homeowners, who had hoped for tunnels in their yard, may have been disappointed, but the archaeology of the alcove provided tangible evidence of the kinds of conditions that escaped slaves endured on their way to freedom.

Another project in Pennsylvania also uncovered a probable hiding place on the Underground Railroad, this one on a site associated with the famous abolitionists Thaddeus Stevens and Lydia Hamilton Smith. The construction of a hotel and convention center complex in Lancaster included several buildings that had been owned by Thaddeus Stevens, the founder of the Republican Party in Pennsylvania, and a well-known antislavery proponent. Among his many actions, Stevens fought to have the Fugitive Slave Law of 1850 repealed and defended participants in the Christiana Resistance, which involved protecting several fugitive slaves from being apprehended (Delle and Levine 2004:134). Lydia Hamilton Smith was African American and was said to be a conductor on the Underground Railroad. She was Stevens' housekeeper and is portrayed as his companion and bedmate in Steven Spielberg's 2012 movie *Lincoln*.

The archaeological investigation focused on possible domestic deposits in two small courtyards that were going to be impacted by the pending convention-center construction: one behind the Stevens house and the other behind the Smith house. While the Smith courtyard was seriously disturbed, the Stevens courtyard had been covered with concrete. Beneath the concrete there was a layer of coal-ash fill dating to the 1860s. The fill covered intact brick pavement that sealed two nineteenth-century cisterns. The largest of the cisterns measured 7 feet 11 inches east–west by 5 feet 10 inches north–south and had a vaulted roof and brick floor. The north and south walls supporting the vault were made of brick, and the east and west walls were made of a mixture of brick and limestone. The eastern wall had been extensively rebuilt, and there were two penetrations through the cistern walls: one in the northeast corner, which connected to a clay-lined gutter that probably brought rainwater or water drawn from a stream into the cistern, and one in the southwest corner, which was eventually surrounded by a rectangular brick structure that probably housed a pump.

A trench had been dug along the rebuilt eastern wall of the cistern sometime between when it ceased to be used for water and when it was filled in the 1890s. A loosely built retaining wall extended from the vault of the cistern toward the foundation wall of the Kleiss Saloon, the building that bordered the courtyard on the east. The archaeologists interpreted the trench as having been dug "to reconfigure the eastern wall of the vaulted cistern." A carelessly bricked-in, roughly square "window" was present in this rebuilt wall and was "just large enough for a person of medium build to fit through" (Delle and

Levine 2004:146–147). There was a corroded iron spittoon standing right next to the window, as if for easy access, and there was a patch over a break in the foundation wall of the Kleiss Saloon, which would have allowed a person to crawl from its cellar into the cistern. Datable artifacts associated with the trench feature—especially Blue-Tinted Molded Ironstone, introduced in 1850 and popular in the following decade—suggest that modifications made to the cistern to adapt it for use as a hiding place dated to the 1850s, which was the time period when Thaddeus Stevens was making modifications to the property. Stevens was out of office between 1853 and 1859, and Delle and Levine suggest that he may have spent those years "actively participating in the Underground Railroad movement from his home base in Lancaster" (2004:148).

Unlike the Parvin alcove, the Stevens cistern did not include artifacts relating to its use as a hiding place. Delle and Levine speculate that escapees probably spent more time in the cellar of the Kleiss Saloon than in the cistern, where they would need to hide only if bounty hunters or a U.S. Marshal was hunting for fugitives on the premises.

Another cellar with possible evidence of Underground Railroad activity was explored in the 1990s in Syracuse, New York. A series of sculpted faces was found on a wall in the cellar of what was originally the Wesleyan Methodist Church; it had been converted into a restaurant and property-title company in recent years. Archaeologists Douglas Armstrong and LuAnn Wurst studied and published an article on the faces in 2003. The seven faces, which had been known for years but were assumed to be the work of a twentieth-century janitor in the building, were located on the walls of a circular enclosure around the furnace at the west end of the original cellar of the church. Possibly to make them invisible from the entrance to the cellar at the east end, they appear to have been placed just beyond a jog in the passageway that led to the west side. Archaeologist Warren Barbour's analysis of fingerprint impressions in the faces concluded that the three from which fingerprints could be lifted had been done by different artists. This finding ruled out a theory that they were all made by the keeper of the furnace to entertain children on Halloween in the early twentieth century.

The best-preserved of the faces had well-defined features, especially the hair, resembling known photographs of Frederick Douglass (Figure 5.4). The date "1817" was scratched in the clay below the face and may or may not have been incised there when the face was originally made (Armstrong and Wurst 2003). The association of the date with the face, however, was surely inten-

Figure 5.4. Modeled clay face (probably Frederick Douglass), found in the basement of the Wesleyan Methodist Church. Courtesy of the Onondaga Historical Association.

tional, as 1817 was the year Frederick Douglass was born. The other faces are less distinct, although all were made by the same method. The artists prepared the wall surface by gouging out oval support forms on the wall and then applying layers of moist clay to build up a surface which could then be molded, sculpted, and smoothed to form facial detail. In at least two cases, black ash had been used to darken the natural clay color for eye color, and the clay was molded into a tight curl pattern characteristic of African American hair. These details are convincing evidence that the faces are meant to represent African Americans. The question was who made them and when.

The context made it seem more than likely that the faces and the cellar passageway in which they were found somehow related to the Underground Railroad. The Wesleyan Methodist Church, completed in 1847, splintered off from the Methodist Episcopal Church "because it would not take an active stand against slavery" (Armstrong and Wurst 2003:19). The new church provided a place for worship of the splinter congregation, many of whom had ties to the Underground Railroad, and it also provided a home for the publication of two newspapers—the *American Wesleyan* and the *True Wesleyan*—both of which were dedicated to the abolition of slavery. Syracuse and much of Central New York were heavily involved in the abolition movement from the 1830s until the outbreak of the Civil War, and the participation of the church as an Underground Railroad station is well documented.

The Wesleyan Methodist Church burned in 1898, but the hand-dug cellar passageway where the faces were located survived the fire. Armstrong and Wurst think that fire damage to at least two of the faces proves that they were there when it happened. The entrance to the cellar passageway was disturbed by a cinderblock wall built in 1957, but beyond that wall the passageway goes through the original east foundation of the church. About 3 m west of the foundation, the passageway jogs to the north around a foundation pier and support beam and then continues in a straight course to the west end of the cellar, where the furnace (and most of the faces) were located. An earthen bench, which had been buried under all sorts of building-related debris when the faces were first investigated, was uncovered on the north side of the passageway. It was 12 feet long by about 1.75 feet wide and could have accommodated several people sitting side by side or someone stretched out to sleep. The proximity of the bench to the furnace would have made it a cozy hiding place.

Three excavation units were placed in the furnace area. Artifacts recovered from an upper level in this area—an ivory piano key and about two-thirds of a glass communion cup—related to the church, but a round brick feature found about 13 cm below the surface appeared to belong to the original wood-burning furnace. Armstrong and Wurst interpreted this feature as evidence that a furnace existed in the basement prior to the 1898 fire. Artifacts associated with the brick feature were sparse but included window glass dating to the 1846–1877 era and a fragment of a black transfer-printed ceramic that was popular in the 1840s and 1850s. There was also a black glass bead.

The evidence is circumstantial, but it does not seem unreasonable to attribute the faces to the work of escapees who found shelter in the basement of the Wesleyan Church. The faces were removed from the former church walls for conservation, a delicate task accomplished by Gary McGowan and Cheryl LaRoche. To qualify for grants to cover the cost of the conservation, ownership was transferred to the National Underground Railroad Freedom Center in Cincinnati, but the local community wanted the faces to stay in Syracuse. They were first exhibited at the Onondaga Historical Society in Syracuse and are now permanently curated there.

Resourcefulness in the Eighteenth Century

Smuggling

Historical archaeologists are in a unique position to find material evidence of smuggling, especially in periods when goods from one place or another were forbidden. The Navigation Acts, which forbade the colonists to ship certain products to anywhere but England and also restricted the importation of goods not loaded in England, were routinely defied in the years before the Revolutionary War (Schmidt and Mrozowski 1988:34). European wines and liquors were "liberally consumed" in Newport, Rhode Island, for instance, even though they were not supposed to be available, and there is plenty of evidence for the importation of ceramics and glass from the Dutch and French colonies in the Caribbean. A major source of non-English goods was the cargo of ships captured by privateers, which, according to archaeologists Peter Schmidt and Stephen Mrozowski, were "a welcome economic boost for the many merchants who financed them" (1988:33). While historians have emphasized the illicit trade in commercial goods (molasses, sugar, rum, and tea) carried on these ships, archaeologists have the opportunity to identify less economically important goods when they recognize them.

By the middle of the eighteenth century, the British successfully blockaded much illicit trade, but the colonists found ways to avoid surveillance, primarily by offloading and loading forbidden products out of sight. A cultural resource management project done along the proposed route of U.S. Route 301 in Delaware uncovered portions of a cartway that belonged to a branch of the Reedy Island Cart Road network, an active smuggling route from the late seventeenth century up to the Revolutionary War. The archaeological investigation was conducted to test a predictive model that had been developed for the entire U.S. Route 301 project area, an area that included 17 miles of new highway in New Castle County (Burrow et al. 2014). This cartway was part of a network of cartways used to carry both illicit and licit goods between the Chesapeake Bay and the Delaware River.

According to Patrick Harshbarger (Hunter Research Inc.), who conducted the historical research for Hunter Research Inc's work on the 301 project, Augustine Hermann was the main player in the establishment of the cart road network in Maryland and Delaware (personal communication, June 28, 2016). This is the same Hermann (also spelled Heermans) whose warehouse was excavated on the Broad Financial Center site on Pearl Street in Lower Manhattan, New York City, in the 1980s. Hermann came to New Amsterdam as the agent for a Dutch mercantile firm in the early 1640s and eventually built his own warehouse on the East River, where he dealt in Hudson River furs, Virginia tobacco, wines, provisions, and enslaved Africans (Cantwell and Wall 2001:154). In the 1650s he left New Amsterdam to turn his attention to a 6,000-acre grant he had received on the Bohemia River in Delaware. There he established Bohemia Manor and apparently began developing the network of cartways that provided convenient routes for smuggling.

The section of the Reedy Island Cart Road that was archaeologically investigated ran through a 250-acre tract of land at the head of Second Drawyer's Creek in St. Georges Hundred, New Castle County (Burrow et al. 2014). The tract was owned by a man named John Taylor and his descendants in the seventeenth century and by Alexander Armstrong and his descendants in the eighteenth century. Hunter Research began the investigation with a geophysical survey that aimed at detecting patterns that might relate to the alignment of a cartway. Parallel linear anomalies seemed to suggest just that, and the archaeologists tested the anomalies with long backhoe trenches. The linear features, which began about 0.75 feet below the plow zone, turned out to be ditches, about 3 feet wide at the top and 1 foot across at the base. The hard-packed berm between the ditches measured 7 to 8 feet across, just wide enough for light, two-wheeled carts, and probably pack animals (Figure 5.5). A line of square or rectangular postholes that had been cut through the berm probably related to a fence that reused the alignment of the earlier cart road after it was no longer a transportation route. The only artifacts recovered from the cartway proper were animal combs.

The archaeologists interpreted the linear ditches as drains for runoff from the berm, which was the actual cartway. No ruts or hoof prints were found on the berm, but subsequent plowing probably destroyed them. The archaeologists calculated that the berm could have accommodated a 4-foot-8.5-inch

Figure 5.5. Excavated stain of the Reedy Island Cart Road uncovered during the U.S. Route 301 cultural resources project in Delaware. Courtesy of Hunter Research, Inc.

wheel separation of cart or wagon axles, and the berm might have been able to accommodate an overall vehicle width of about 7 feet for a Conestoga wagon (Burrow et al. 2014). If boats were transported on the cartways, as had been documented on another cartway in the network, the ditches would have served as guides for sled runners.

Although research did not locate written records relating to illicit trade on the Reedy Island Cart Road, the investigators claim that smuggling along the cartway involved ships either lying in anchorage off Reedy Island or calling on the Appoquinimink Creek to avoid customs agents in Philadelphia (Burrow et al. 2014:2–3) (Figure 5.5). Reedy Island was the most sheltered anchorage on the Delaware Bay, and it stayed ice free in the winter. Partial cargoes could be offloaded there without having to pay fees and then go on to Philadelphia. In the other direction, cargoes could be transported back across St. Georges Hundred to the Chesapeake, thereby avoiding the import duties of the more tightly regulated Maryland and Virginia ports. Among the lucrative products moved in this way was tobacco, which otherwise would have been subject to the regulation of the Navigation Acts.

Merchants also found ways to avoid paying import and export fees in Rhode Island. Illicit goods delivered by ships from the West Indies or Europe were offloaded in places as far afield as Martha's Vineyard and Nantucket and then transported on small fishing boats that could sneak into Newport undetected (Schmidt and Mrozowski 1988). Although it has not been specifically documented, it is not unlikely that New Brunswick and Raritan Landing in New Jersey outstripped Perth Amboy, the legal entry port for East Jersey, because there were no customs officials to prevent illicit activities at these smaller ports.

Figuring out what was illicitly acquired and what was legally acquired appears to have been a considerably more difficult problem in the Spanish colonies. According to Kathleen Deagan (2007:99), "Spain's colonial economic policies . . . rendered illicit commerce a normal part of people's daily life and cultural practice in the Americas." Spain required that her colonies send all their raw materials to the home country and that the colonies use only manufactured goods produced in Spain. The intended balance of trade did not work, though, because Spain was consistently unable to provide the manufactured goods needed, which drove colonists to turn to illicit trade with foreigners to survive. Crediting Carl Halbirt for the research, Deagan (2007:100) cites archaeological evidence for the practice of illegal trade between St. Augustine's residents and the English as early as 1670 and suggests there was a steady increase in the use of foreign goods throughout the eighteenth century.

Although Spain prohibited trade between its American colonies on English, Dutch, and French merchant ships, it did not prohibit the purchase of goods manufactured in those countries as long as they arrived on Spanish-licensed ships. Spanish economic historians have estimated that by 1700 only about 5% of the goods shipped from Cádiz (including wine, oil, some cloth, wax, and iron) were of Spanish origin (Deagan 2007:101). Legal foreign goods also entered via ships permitted to call in Mexico as part of the slave-trade *asiento* (contract) and through the sale of cargoes captured through Spanish privateering, especially after ca. 1730 (Deagan 2007:101–102). The problem is to distinguish items that entered legally from items that entered illegally.

To look at this problem, Deagan reexamined the contents of 124 undisturbed contexts from six domestic sites that represent a cross section of St. Augustine's eighteenth-century households by income, ethnic origin, and occupation. Her study concluded that more English wares were present as the eighteenth century progressed, beginning in the 1735–1740 time frame and increasing even more in the 1745–1750 time frame, when they would have been illegal (2007:107). With one exception, the more well-to-do households in the sample consistently had more Spanish wares than non-Spanish ones, but the poorest household had more English-made wares, which were illegal. The exception was the household of a harbor guard that consistently had more non-Spanish wares than Spanish ones, perhaps because as a customs guard he would have had easy access to them (Deagan 2007:112). His household had high proportions of both English and French tableware ceramics through the eighteenth century. Deagan considers illicit economic behavior a "quintessential" historical archaeological issue, because it requires the articulation of text-generated and archaeologically deposited evidence to learn something neither source alone could reveal (2007:113).

Pirates

The English (and Spanish) colonists' avoidance of trade restrictions is surely an example of resistance to control from abroad. The pirates and privateers themselves were outlaws. Their participation in illicit trade was not so much resistance as opportunism—what might be seen as agency in the extreme. Although there are plenty of published tales of piracy, there is little actual material evidence in the Americas. Just one recovered shipwreck, found off the coast of Cape Cod, has been definitively connected to pirates, although a second (this one found in Beaufort Inlet on the coast of North Carolina) has been attributed to Blackbeard, the most famous pirate of all (Wilde-Ramsing and Carnes-McNaughton 2016:31, 35).

The wreck of the *Whydah*, found 500 feet off Marconi Beach in Cape Cod in 1983, lay in 20 to 30 feet of water under as much as 20 feet of loose, shifting sand on a cobble-strewn stratum of clay (Hamilton 2006:131). The project to recover its remains was initially financed by Maritime Explorations, Inc., a private group of investors. The involvement of treasure hunters in the search for pirate ships has caused a good deal of consternation in the archaeological community. As stated by Charles Ewen in the introduction to *X Marks the Spot*, a book about the archaeology of piracy, the conundrum is "should an archaeologist work with the commercial collector to salvage as much information as possible before the artifact collection is sold and dispersed or does collaboration tacitly endorse and legitimize the activities of the collector and encourage them to mine even more sites?" (Ewen 2006:6). In the case of the *Whydah*, professionals Rolland Betts and Tom Bernstein worked in a joint venture with Maritime Explorations (MEI) with the approval of the state and federal government, and much of the collection, now estimated at 106,000 artifacts, has been professionally studied (Page and Ewen 2016:261).

The identity of the wreck was confirmed early in the project when the bell, or at least one of the ship's bells, was recovered. The inscription on the bell reads, THE + WHYDAH + GALLEY + 1716. According to historical records, the *Whydah* was built in London as a slave ship. In 1716 it sailed from England to the Gold Coast of Ghana and the slave market town, *Whydah*, to collect its cargo. The slaves were sold in Jamaica. In February of 1717, the ship was headed home loaded with sugar, indigo, quinine, and the silver and gold specie earned from the sale of the Africans, when it was intercepted by the pirate Samuel Bellamy. Bellamy and his crew exchanged their own ship for the *Whydah* and its valuable cargo and headed up the coast of North America. They were aiming for Richmond Island, which is now in the state of Maine, but they never arrived there. The ship got caught on a shoal and capsized in April of 1717, stranding 130 to 200 men and between £20,000 and £30,000 in silver and gold.

The rich artifact assemblage recovered from the *Whydah* site included personal things—silver, pewter and brass buttons, cufflinks, and buckles—and the archaeologists plotted their distribution to look for patterning. The more valuable silver apparel items were found in the stern, where, they speculated, the ship's captain, quartermaster, and other officers would have resided. There were also pewter plates, some with cut marks and graffiti cut into them. The "A" on one of them may have been someone's initial or possibly an early depiction of the Freemason Compass and Square (Hamilton 2006:157). There were tools—mauls, caulking chisels, crow's-foot pry bars, awls, hammers, and vises—indicating the level of carpentry and blacksmithing practiced, as well as navigational implements—ring dial, charting compasses, and a stylus—relating to the sailing of the ship. Not surprisingly, many of the finds related to ordnance. There were dozens of cannons, guns, swords, and other weapons. The treasure consisted mainly of Spanish silver *real* coins, some with holes drilled in them (Kinkor 2016:230), and chipped African (Akan) gold jewelry.

Although there is still no definitive artifact that connects the shipwreck found in Beaufort's Inlet, North Carolina, with Blackbeard's flagship, *Queen Anne's Revenge* (that is, no bell with a name on it), Mark U. Wilde-Ramsing and Charles R. Ewen present a convincing argument in a summary article published in 2012. The wreck was found by Intersal Inc., treasure salvors searching for a Spanish treasure ship in 1996 (Page and Ewen 2016:261). Initial documentary research and a process of elimination pointed to the identification of the wreck as *Queen Anne's Revenge*, which was known to have gone aground in Beaufort's Inlet in 1718. Early artifact finds, including a brass bell dating to 1705 and early eighteenth-century ordnance, were consistent with the attribution, making it a potentially very important find. Intersal Inc. agreed to turn the project over to the North Carolina Underwater Archaeology Branch to keep the collection intact for the people of North Carolina. The resulting investigation involved a mixed group of private, academic, and state personnel.

The 25-by-15-foot wreck lay 23 feet below mean sea level about 1,500 yards west of the present shipping channel of Beaufort Inlet, which has been navigable since 1672. Initially the artifacts collected mainly related to the ship and its arms, including 15 cannons, a cluster of cannonballs, three large anchors, a grappling hook, numerous iron cask hoops, several rigging elements, and a large amount of ballast stone and concretions (Wilde-Ramsing 2006:168). Subsequent work has exposed much of the ship's hull, more cannons, and many artifacts that tie the wreck to its French origins and ultimately to Blackbeard. Edward Teach, aka Blackbeard, is known to have captured the French vessel *La Concorde* in late 1717 (Wilde-Ramsing 2006:191). *La Concorde* was originally built as a privateer for use in Queen Anne's War (1701–1713) and was put into service as a slave trader after the war. It made three voyages from Africa, one in 1713, another in 1715, and the fatal one in 1717, when Blackbeard captured the ship in Martinique in the West Indies. Components of leg shackles are one of the things that point to its slave trader history (Wilde-Ramsing and Carnes-McNaughton 2016:31). There was also a glass bead thought to be from Ghana or the west coast of Africa.

An early analysis (Lusardi 2006) of the small artifacts recovered—things like pewter plates, wine bottles, tin-glazed ceramics, clay-pipe stems and bowls—did not identify a French connection, but analysis by others (Wilde-Ramsing and Carnes-McNaughton 2016) makes a strong case for one. Lusardi identified only one clearly French-made artifact, a urethral syringe; others, he thought, were mainly English made. Wilde-Ramsing and Carnes-McNaughton, however, analyzed a much larger collection which was recovered from a stratified sample of 5-by-5-foot units (a total of 224) excavated between 2005 and 2012. While 36% of the artifacts analyzed were English, 26% turned out to be French. Among the French-made artifacts were distinctive blue-green windowpanes and flacon bottles dating to the early eighteenth century, French-style copper kettles, large storage jars similar to an example found on the 1717 French shipwreck at St. Melos, a bowl rim of a green-glazed earthenware probably made in the Saintonge region of France, and another small plate coated with a green glaze over a white slip that was probably also made in Saintonge (Wilde-Ramsing and Carnes-McNaughton 2016:41). Various maker's marks indicated French manufacture—a cylinder mark on a clyster (a large pump syringe), indicating that it was made in Rouen; initials on nested weight cups representing the town of Montpelier; and a porringer marked "IM" and "DV," probably made in Metz (Wilde-Ramsing and Carnes-McNaughton 2016:48). The attention to these French-made artifacts and many others was particularly important for the definite identification of the wreck as that of the former *La Concorde*.

The artifact analysis of the French-made artifacts done by Wilde-Ramsing and Carnes-McNaughton provides at least a partial picture of the lifestyle of some of the French sailors who remained on board the *Concorde* after it had been abducted by Teach. Besides the ceramics, they describe the medical instruments found—lancets for bleeding, porringers for bleeding basins, glass cups, clysters, syringes, saws, picks, surgical knives, pliers, forceps, probes, extractors, needles, gut for suturing, and straps—and speculate that they belonged to Dubois, Bourgneuf, and Deshayes, who were identified as the surgeons on the ship. They propose that the silver buckles and gilded buttons found might have come from their clothes: even as captured men, they would have had status among the crew and would have dressed accordingly. The decorative, short, distinctively French swords or dirks found might also have been theirs, and it was probably they who ate from Saintonge tablewares rather than the indelicate pewter plates that served the rest of the crew.

The archaeologists who have studied these two pirate ships have tried to use the artifacts to interpret the lives of the pirates on board, but it is difficult "because pirates differ from merchants primarily in the legality of their actions" (Page and Ewen 2016:260). Courtney Page and Charles Ewen, however, propose that even if the artifacts aren't very different, the quantities of them may be. To test this idea, they compared five categories of artifacts from the *Whydah* and *Queen Anne's Revenge* with the same categories from the *Henrietta Marie*, a slave ship that ran aground off Key West in Florida in 1700, and the HMS *Invincible*, a French-built naval ship that ran aground off the coast of England in the middle of the eighteenth century. The categories for comparison were arms and armament, personal effects, cargo (container, treasure, jewelry, commodity, community use), kitchen, and tools and instruments. Not surprisingly, arms and armaments exceeded 80% for the two pirate ships and the naval ship, thus revealing no real difference between them. Even the slave ship had more than 40% in that category. The two pirate ships, however, had more in the cargo category than either the naval or slave ship, and the *Queen Anne's Revenge* had more (over 20%) than the *Whydah* (about 15%), probably explained by the fact that *Whydah* was torn apart, all but two of the crew dying, while the *Queen Anne's Revenge* was just run aground. Blackbeard's crew conceivably walked away with whatever they could carry.

There are lots of problems with this study, which the authors point out. The artifact assemblages were different sizes, the ships operated at different times, and they sailed to different locations (Page and Ewen 2016:268). There were also the differing conditions of the shipwrecks, in addition to how much scavenging and salvaging had taken place before controlled recovery was attempted. While the cargo category surely distinguishes the pirate assemblages from the others, no other patterns were discernible.

Acts of defiance may be clandestine, but they are done, for the most part, in public places, that is, away from home. They are not so much about vulnerability as they are about escaping various constraints—of a job, of the law, of confinement of one sort or another. Finding a material record of these acts almost seems unfair. They got away with them in life, but we have caught them in the act archaeologically. Other kinds of clandestine acts are done for private purposes in private places. The next chapter looks at the archaeological evidence for these kinds of acts—expressions of identity, individuality, vulnerability. Through uncovering and interpreting these kinds of acts, we are able to strip away at least some of the anonymity of people in the past.

6

Clandestine Pursuits

Private Spaces

The previous chapter dealt with clandestine actions that incidentally left evidence behind. In this chapter we look at objects we have dug up that were meant to be hidden. Intentionally hidden objects have special meanings for individuals. In uncovering them we enter the worlds of past people and attempt, albeit inadequately, to enter their minds. Henry Glassie (1988) has written much about the importance of biography in the historical endeavor, of knowing all different kinds of people. Every mind is complex; every mind has secrets. In the absence of written words from the past, archaeologists employ objects, and in them we embed meaning. "To allow a voice to the people of the past, we must put tongues in inanimate objects" (Glassie 1988:86). Although this is unavoidably the nature of the archaeological endeavor, it seems particularly challenging when trying to understand purposefully hidden things. Unlike a hammer, which Glassie uses to demonstrate how even such a useful tool leads to a complex of meanings ("it demands more and more nails, more iron, more mines and miners, more ironmongers, more immigrants" [1988:86]), a scratched cross on a ceramic pot or a folded coin is meant to be symbolic, its meaning is intentionally hidden, not merely overlooked for lack of imagination. The problem for us is to arrive at meanings on which we can agree and that make sense.

In her book *On Longing*, Susan Stewart (1993) explores the power of narratives associated with "the miniature, the gigantic, the souvenir, and the collection." Objects are animated by their personal associations. A souvenir, for instance, "speaks to a context of origin through a language of longing, for it is not an object arising out of need or use value; it is an object arising out of the necessarily insatiable demands of nostalgia" (Stewart 1993:135). What is relevant here is how inconsequential the object may be—a plastic Eiffel

Tower, a ribbon from a corsage—and still contain so much evocative power. Like the mundane objects discussed in this chapter, souvenirs require narratives to give them meaning. "The souvenir displaces the point of authenticity as it itself becomes the point of origin for narrative. Such a narrative cannot be generalized to encompass the experience of anyone; it pertains only to the possessor of the object" (Stewart 1993:136). The emphasis on individuality is important here. Mundane objects that have been endowed with meaning connect to individual people and the archaeologically elusive complexity of their lives.

Scratched Messages in Windowpanes

Graffiti boldly displayed in public places more often than not conveys messages meant for the multitudes, for example, "I love Sarah," "Elect Obama," "End the war." Messages scratched into windowpanes are different. They are hard to read and must surely have been meant to be secret. Such a message was deciphered on pieces of glass recovered from a privy owned by a cutler, Benjamin Humphreys, and his wife, Mary, in Revolutionary-period Philadelphia. The Humphreys, or maybe just Mary, ran a tavern out of their house, although it was never formally licensed. There were no children in the cutler's family, so the message scratched in the window was presumably put there by an adult, perhaps a tavern regular. The message reads, "We admire riches, And are in love with i . . ." The site was excavated by John Milner Associates, and Juliette Gerhardt, the firm's laboratory director, determined that the quote came from a fragment of a sentence uttered by the Roman senator Marcus Portius Cato, better known to history as Cato the Younger. The incomplete last word of the quote is "idleness." According to Gerhardt (2016:77), the sentence came from a speech that Cato made to the senate in 63 BCE concerning the fate of a group of conspirators who had plotted to overthrow the Republic. It followed a speech by Julius Caesar, and both speeches were recorded by the Roman historian Sallust and translated into English by schoolmaster John Clarke in 1734. Parts of the translation were used by the political writer and pamphleteer Thomas Gordon in a series of articles critiquing the British political system, which may have been familiar to Philadelphians. Cato's ideas were made popular in the play *Cato, a Tragedy*, by Joseph Addison, supposedly a favorite of George Washington, who had it performed for the soldiers during the winter at Valley Forge.

Figure 6.1. Glass fragment with scratched name "Boudinot," found below the window of a dependency behind Morven, the house of Richard and Annis Stockton, Princeton, New Jersey.

Several names were also scratched in the tavern window: Finney, de Haas, WM, all identifiable residents of the nearby neighborhood, and presumably regular drinkers at the Humphreys' establishment. Window glass with names scratched into it has also been found elsewhere. At Morven, in Princeton, New Jersey, a fragment of glass was recovered that clearly read "Boudinot" (Figure 6.1). Morven was the home of Richard Stockton, a signer of the Declaration of Independence, and his wife, Annis. Boudinot was Annis Stockton's maiden name, and her brother Elias Boudinot was the president of the Second Continental Congress in Philadelphia from 1782 to 1783. It seems unlikely that he scratched his name in his married sister's window, and equally unlikely that she scratched it there. Perhaps it was done by a child who looked up to his or her uncle or by a female member of the household who secretly admired him.

Another Revolutionary War–period example is a windowpane with the words "Peace forms o_" elegantly scratched in it. Reported by Diana George of the New York City consulting company Crysallis, perhaps the words celebrated the end of the war or, at least, the wished-for end. The fragment came from fill removed from a boat slip while monitoring utilities work at the South Street Seaport in New York City.

Concealed Objects in the English Tradition

More common than scratched messages in windowpanes are concealed objects endowed with magical qualities. Even though things concealed above ground aren't commonly the domain of archaeologists, a special issue of the journal *Historical Archaeology*, published in 2014 and dedicated to Ralph Merrifield, included studies that describe and interpret hidden objects, especially objects hidden inside houses. Shoes hidden behind walls near chimneys and doors, a practice that has an English precedent dating to the Middle Ages, are fairly common. In that context they are believed to protect the home, especially at vulnerable places like chimneys and doors where, people believed, evil spirits could enter (Costello 2014:36).

The concealed shoes found are generally well worn and thought to resemble their former owners, even children. M. Chris Manning, one of the editors of the special issue, claims there are 123 known examples of shoe concealments in the United States, 57 of them belonging to children (Manning 2014:59). In the same journal, Jessica Costello discusses 44 boots and shoes found at the John Adams Birthplace in Quincy, Massachusetts (Costello 2014:35–51). They appear to date to the period 1800–1830, during which time the house was occupied by shoemakers. Costello speculates that the hidden shoes might have related to their trade, but it is also possible that there, and elsewhere, they had other meanings, for example, to protect a home from evil spirits or to commemorate family events.

The tradition of using witch bottles to cause bewitchment can also be traced to the Middle Ages in England, although in the United States they have generally been associated with African American contexts. According to Manning (2014:53), "the effectiveness of a witch bottle relied on the physical connection thought to exist between a witch or wizard and victim." The bottle had to contain urine from a victim who was suffering from illness or injury due to bewitchment, especially urinary or kidney problems, such as nephritis, bladder infections, kidney stones, and epilepsy or fits. Bent pins, nails, or other sharp objects presumably meant to cause pain and difficulty when urinating were sometimes mixed with the urine. According to Manning, fewer than a dozen documented examples of witch bottles are known in the United States. Many more than a dozen bottles found archaeologically, however, have been considered as possible witch bottles.

A dark green wine bottle found neatly tucked into a niche in the basement of an early eighteenth-century house foundation at Raritan Landing in New Jersey appeared to be a good candidate for a witch bottle, especially since two copper nodules and a slightly bent straight pin were recovered nearby (Figure 6.2). Chemical testing of the bottle's contents, however, did not identify urine, and the URS archaeologists who excavated the site were not convinced that the bottle had spiritual meaning (Yamin 2011:37). Likewise, Matthew Reeves (2009) did not conclude that the bottles "concealed" in the basement of the oldest part of the James Madison plantation house in Montpelier, Virginia, had spiritual significance. As described by Reeves, the cellar spaces were primarily used by the Madisons' enslaved workers for cooking, preparing foods for long-term storage, socializing, and resting "out of sight of the house's white occupants" (Reeves 2009). A concrete floor laid in 1901 covered nineteenth-century surfaces, but when the floors were lifted, archaeologists completely excavated the spaces beneath them. While evidence of storage pits, wall partitions, old flooring, and various features relating to daily activities was uncovered, there did not appear to be any caches of possible spiritual objects.

Figure 6.2. Possible "witch" bottle, Raritan Landing, New Jersey. From Yamin 2011:Figure 3.11.

Parts of three bottles, however, were found in "secret" places. One of them consisted of the lip of a wine bottle that had been stuck inside and under a brick wall. When several bricks were removed from the wall, the base and neck of the bottle became visible, along with a couple of shattered bone fragments and three broken eggshells. Reeves thought that the bottle's context was unusual, because it would have been necessary to excavate part of the clay floor and remove bricks to create the cavity that concealed it. The niche was on the outside wall of the secure storage area, where only the most trusted slaves were allowed to go. Another partial wine bottle was found concealed in the brick wall inside the secure storage area, and the two niches were connected, making it possible to pass a wine bottle beneath the wall of the secure storage area into the adjacent workroom. This practical purpose seemed a more probable explanation for the concealment than a spiritual one, and Reeves thought it was more likely a method of resistance than an indication of spiritual practice. He makes the point that to interpret it as an example of spiritual practice would "miss the opportunity of it representing a means for slaves to resist the restrictions placed on the secure storage room of the cellar" (Reeves 2009). Slaves who were admitted could pass things out to slaves who were not admitted to the secure area.

Another bottle, this one for medicine, was found at the base of a chimney in a subfloor pit at the north corner of the north cellar room in the Montpelier basement. Chimneys as well as doorways are places often considered vulnerable. The bottle was placed upright in one of several rectangular ash pits located in this part of the cellar. It was filled with charred material, similar to filling described elsewhere in the ethnohistorical literature. Reeves did not attempt to attribute spiritual or any other meaning to this find. He found that unlike the bottles inside and outside the storeroom, there was not enough context to interpret it at all (Reeves 2009). Bottles found archaeologically that do meet the criteria for genuine witch bottles are described in a summary article by Laurie Wilkie (1997:89). They include examples from the walls of slave cabin sites in North Carolina and Virginia and also from beneath the floors of slave cabins at the Hermitage plantation in Tennessee.

Another category of artifact that has been interpreted as having spiritual significance is an altered coin, sometimes pierced, sometimes bent or folded. Early archaeological finds of pierced coins, in particular, seemed to be consistently from African American sites, although, as with witch bottles, there is an English precedent. According to Michael T. Lucas (2014:107), "perforated coins were used by the English for working magic and preventing harm at least as far back as the sixteenth century." In America pierced silver coins have been recovered from archaeological sites in Virginia, Georgia, Louisiana, and Arkansas. Worn around the neck or ankle on a string, they were supposedly for "turning away evil" (Wilkie 1997:89). James Davidson (2004) has argued that in addition to being altered and made of silver, late sixteenth-century three- and sixpence coins were particularly powerful because of the cross design on them.

Although Davidson (2004:22) thinks the assumption that "pierced coins are entirely African derived is erroneous," his own work at the Freedman's Town Cemetery (1869–1907) in Dallas, Texas, provided clear evidence for the use of coin charms by enslaved Africans and their descendants. Freedman's Town was founded in 1869 by a community of formerly enslaved people. Coins spanning all time periods were recovered from 29 of the 1,150 burials that were excavated. Fifteen of the coins were perforated and were associated with the neck or ankle, which Davidson notes is "reminiscent of charms known from folk belief accounts and indicative of everyday objects charged and imbued with attributes for supernatural control" (Davidson 2004:23).

More unusual than pierced coins in archaeological contexts are folded ones. Examples have been found in Anglican contexts in Virginia and Maryland (Cofield 2014:94). According to Cofield, bent silver coins had supernatural powers as amulets to protect dairies, in particular, from the effects of witch-craft. They have been found in many contexts, however, and it is not easy to know their specific meaning. Cofield mentions a ca. 1619–1625 bent James I penny from Flowerdew Hundred, a ca. 1583–1603 Elizabeth I sixpence from the Sandys site, a ca. 1610–1619 Dutch two-*stuiver* coin from James Fort, and a ca. 1582–1584 Elizabeth I sixpence from the Reverend Richard Buck site. All these sites are in Virginia. She proposes that the location of the coin in an unfinished pithouse or cellar at Flowerdew, along with the neck of a Bellarmine jar and ceramic sherd repurposed as a funnel, might mean the pit was used as a dairy. Recessed pits on seventeenth-century sites are often interpreted as dairies, be-cause they would stay cooler than structures at or above ground level.

The coin found in the burial at the Reverend Richard Buck site came from one of nine burials. The burial with the coin was the only one that included grave goods and had not been wrapped in a shroud. It was one of two with the head placed at the east end, instead of the west, which was customary for a Christian burial. This mark of disrespect seems inconsistent with the presence of the coin, which is often associated with some kind of magic or power. If the deceased was suspected of sorcery or cunning, the coin might have been placed in the grave as an amulet to prevent his or her spirit from rising to harm the living (Cofield 2014:99). It is notable that bent coins appear consistently at sites dating to the late sixteenth or early seventeenth century.

James Davidson (2004:31) has argued that archaeologists may have too readily attributed amulets and such to Native Americans and African Americans because of a desire to "exoticize" black culture and society, and the need to "other" them in white society. Manning (2014) has made the same point, although his coedited volume about the archaeology and material culture of folk religion goes a long way to challenging this perspective. In response to a thread on the list Histarch in the spring of 2015, Manning summarized the kinds of materials that have been found deliberately concealed in eighteenth- and nineteenth-century dwellings in the United States. In addition to those already discussed, he mentions doll-like figurines, garments, iron objects (horseshoes, knives, hoe blades, etc.), Bibles, fragments of hymnals and almanacs, the desiccated bodies of cats, inscribed marks such as the so-called daisy wheel and Marian symbols, bifaces and other prehistoric lithic artifacts, and spoons (usually silver). Manning also mentions a large collection of chickens found in the wall of one house and horse skulls reported in buildings at South Deerfield, Massachusetts; and Cahokia, Illinois. It is also here that he argues that "concealing ritualized objects in buildings among Euro-Americans is more widespread than many of us may realize, as up to this point most of the focus has been on African-American traditions" (Manning 2015). There are clearly too many finds to describe in detail, but Manning maintains an informal database that he may make widely available. What is absolutely clear is that Americans from many different backgrounds continued practices in their New World homes that involved concealing objects to achieve supernatural ends.

African American Pots, Pipes, and Caches

Careful analysis of context is essential to interpreting finds associated with spiritual practice, and a number of American archaeologists have written about its importance. Laurie Wilkie (1997:84) claims that in a plantation context, "the secret maintenance of magical practices was not merely a means of exerting control over circumstances of life or of resisting planter authority, beliefs in magic and magical practices also persisted because they were intrinsic to the ways in which enslaved Africans defined themselves, their families, and their relationship to life, death, and the world around them." In her 1997 article, Wilkie presents archaeological examples of African American spiritual traditions from three geographical regions (South Carolina, the Chesapeake, and Louisiana), and she shows how the application of a diachronic model in these areas could enlighten our understanding of African American belief systems.

Her first example is from South Carolina, where Leland Ferguson interpreted decorative motifs found on Colono Ware pottery bowls as representing Bakongo African motifs. Ferguson described the motifs as cosmograms consisting of "localized incisions and scratches that might be placed on the bottom of the vessel, out of sight of the casual user, or scratched into a finished vessel, marring its potter's smoothed or burnished finish" (Ferguson 1999:117). One line of the cross, Ferguson believes, represents the boundary between the world of the living and that of the dead, and the other represents a path leading across the boundary. Most of the vessels (18 out of 28) cataloged by Ferguson came from underwater sites, which is consistent with Bakongo beliefs that "explain the earth, the land of the living, as a mountain over a watery barrier that separates this world from the land of the dead beneath" (Ferguson 1999:118). According to Ferguson, the Colono Ware bowls bearing crosses, and crosses contained in circles, were made by African Americans and might have been used for sacred medicines. It is also possible that the bowls were used for other magical materials, including stones, white clay, animal remains, shells, broken glass beads. While the clay bowls disappear from the archaeological record about 1800, Wilkie has pointed out that their disappearance does not necessarily mean that the practice of using clay bowls for the preparation of sacred medicine disappeared as well. American- or European-produced ceramics could have been used later for the same purpose.

Since Ferguson pointed out the possible cosmogram motif, other archaeologists have found examples among previously ignored artifacts. In their book about New York City, for instance, Cantwell and Wall (2001:240) describe an eighteenth-century pewter spoon with several Xs or crosses scratched into its bowl found at the bottom of the East River (Figure 13.11 in Cantwell and Wall 2001). Its watery provenience is suggestive. The find was made on the Assay site, which included a complex of wooden wharf structures built into the river bottom.

A second example mentioned by Wilkie (1997) is from the Chesapeake area, where distinctively decorated terra-cotta tobacco pipes have been found on sites dating between 1640 and 1720. Matthew Emerson's analysis of the pipes found that the combination of stamped characters, decorative lines, and white inlay was "almost identical" to decorative techniques used on West African artifacts (Emerson 1999:59–60). He compared various motifs found on Chesapeake pipes to motifs found in Africa—one used to symbolize cattle and herding, another like one found on Asante black earthenware, and a double-bell or double-gong motif like one used on a Cameroonian pipe. Most distinctive, however, was the Kwardata motif, which Emerson claimed was "an exact replication of a West African decorative motif" (1999:60). It consists of a "blank diamond-shaped motif in a band offset on a textured background" and appears on Nigerian pottery, including ritual beer vessels (1999:60). Wilkie interprets the transference of the motif from pottery to tobacco pipes as a possible "substitute for the ritual associated with the traditional beer vessels" (Wilkie 1997:99), the point being that a diachronic perspective contributes to understanding the meaning of the motif. She also notes that these potentially African American–made pipes disappear around the same time that Colono Ware pots appear in this region.

Implied by both Ferguson's and Emerson's interpretations of African motifs on objects made by enslaved Africans on American plantations is that the makers were secretly incorporating magical properties into objects used in daily life. These interpretations have, however, been questioned by many scholars who believe that the objects were probably made by Native Americans (Mouer et al. 1999). While these scholars do not attempt to dispute the Bakongo motif on Colono Ware, they propose that it is more likely that the pots were made by Native Americans than enslaved Africans. As for the pipes, they argue convincingly that the motifs on the pipes have Native American precedents.

Using Louisiana as her third example, Wilkie suggests that contact between previously isolated African American populations led to a transformative stage, with African Americans in Louisiana adopting artifacts similar to those used by enslaved people in Virginia and Maryland for magical uses. In addition, she mentions mixtures of Christian saints and rosary beads found in odd contexts that suggest to Wilkie "the adoption of Catholic iconography for magical use" in what is possibly an example of syncretism (1997:100). There are also reports of hearth areas in slave cabins where coins, beads, shells, buttons, and smooth stones were found and may have served as "ceremonial centers" (Wilkie 1997:100). In Maryland, Mark Leone and colleagues have reported caches of potentially sacred artifacts associated with hearths and the northeast corners of rooms in the basements of eighteenth-century houses in Annapolis. In this case, discussed in detail below, the finds are not interpreted as a continuation of religious traditions from Africa, but rather as an example of creolization. As Wilkie has pointed out, by the time the caches were placed, the majority of the enslaved population of North America consisted of the second generation, that is, not of people who had come from Africa but of their descendants.

The careful examination of context was essential to the interpretation of the caches in Annapolis. Three caches were found in the Charles Carroll House: one under the floor of a ground-floor room in the northeast corner of the house, a huge crystal under the kitchen hearth, and a set of three crystals under the threshold of one of the small rooms. According to an expert in West African art, all of them represent "spirit bundles" whose origins were West African (Leone 2005:202–203). In this tradition the opaque color of crystals looked like the water through which the spirits of dead relatives traveled "home," back to the sea from which they ultimately came (Leone 2005:203). In addition to 14 rock crystals, the cache in the northeast corner of the ground floor room included one-half dozen white bone discs about 0.5 inches in diameter, a smooth black pebble, two coins dated 1790 and 1810, the bottom of a bowl with a blue asterisk on it, and some straight pins (Figure 6.3). The basement rooms where

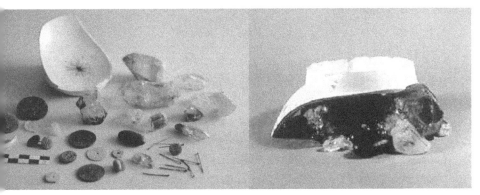

Figure 6.3. Spirit bundle found at the Charles Carroll House, Annapolis, Maryland. Courtesy of Mark Leone, University of Maryland.

they were found belonged to Charles Carroll's cook, Grace, who, Leone says, protected her environment with these ritual bundles and may even have worshipped through them (Leone 2005:204).

Seven caches were uncovered in the basement of Slayton House, across the street from the Carroll House in Annapolis. Parts of a porcelain doll, a ring, pins, and a button were found under the kitchen hearth; pins with a pierced Chinese coin were found in the northeast corner near a doorpost; and a painted bottle filled with solidified black material was buried in a niche in the northeast corner of the new kitchen under its floor. Similar caches of similar objects have since been discovered throughout the American South near chimneys, doors, pipes, stairs, and in northeast corners, where harmful or hurtful spirits could gain entrance in houses and workplaces associated with slaves (Leone 2005:206).

What is missing from this discussion is what these practices mean. It is one thing to recognize that objects relate to magical practices, but quite another to interpret their purpose. According to Ferguson, the cosmograms on Colono Ware (and by others on other objects) "have been used in Central Africa to represent the relationship of the living with the dead and with God and to symbolize centering or harmony with the universe, and historians have shown that similar symbols have been used in the Caribbean and the Americas" (Ferguson 1999:126). Whether that was their meaning in South Carolina is unclear. As Ferguson points out, the cross was also an important symbol for Christians (the crucifix) and for Native Americans of the Southeast (cardinal points); for them it had other meanings. Perhaps, as Laurie Wilkie has said, magical practices did not have specific meanings (or purposes) but were intrinsic to how enslaved Africans defined themselves.

Child's Play

It is not surprising that children would practice clandestine behavior. What is surprising is how little archaeology has looked at children in a serious way. A number of archaeologists, and other scholars as well, have noted that like women, children have been left out, relegated to "a separate sphere from the political, economic, techno-environmental concerns that are seen as the principal preoccupations of traditional and, some would say, andro-centric approaches to the past" (Prangnell and Quirk 2009:38). Historical archaeologists have looked at toys, especially as they relate to bringing up children to have proper middle-class values and gender behavior (Calvert 1992; Fitts 1999; Wall 1991), but we have not looked at toys from a child's point of view. Jane Eva Baxter's work (2005a, 2005b), begun with her doctoral research, attempted to correct this gap in archaeological studies of the past by figuring out how to recognize places in the landscape where children played.

Citing studies by the psychologist David Sobel, Baxter points out that cross-cultural research has shown that secret spaces are a "universal feature of childhood" (Baxter 2005b:71). They are created indoors and outdoors and require only that they give the child the ability to look out on the world without others looking in (Baxter 2005b:72). The problem for archaeologists is to find them. Baxter's own study used five different sites: an orphanage in Albany, New York; a farmhouse in Michigan; a plantation in Louisiana; an upper-class rural residence in Indiana; and a family home-boardinghouse-residence-saloon complex in Virginia City, Nevada. With one exception (the Virginia City complex), she found that children "create identifiable and interpretable patterns in the archaeological record" (Baxter 2005b:73).

Baxter describes the investigation at the Felton farmhouse in Michigan in some detail in her book (2005b). One hundred sixty-five shovel tests and nine 1-by-1-m excavation units were used to test the two acres closest to the farmhouse. A total of 2,666 nonstructural artifacts was recovered, including 37 children's artifacts, particularly toys and parts from children's clothing. Maps of the overall distribution of materials showed that the children's artifacts were clustered in three areas: a 20-by-20-m area in the northern portion of the farmyard near the garden and animal pens, an area directly adjacent to the north side of the farmhouse, and in another area in the extreme northwest corner of the property, where four children's artifacts were found in two adjacent shovel tests. She interpreted the artifacts found near the garden and animal pens as probably related to children's tasks in those areas, and the artifacts near the north side of the house as an area where children might have played without being underfoot but could still be supervised by adults. The artifacts found in the northwest corner of the property, however, were in an area that was an orchard in the nineteenth century and may "represent a secret or special place of childhood where children went to play away from adult supervision" (Baxter 2005b:78). Thus, even though the 37 artifacts relating to children constituted barely 1% of the nonstructural artifact total, Baxter was able to make children visible—at both work and play.

The small numbers of artifacts directly attributable to children are surely one of the factors that have made it so difficult to identify children archaeologically. Studies that focus on middle-class child-rearing using gender-specific artifacts—for example, tea sets and dolls for girls, balls and marbles for boys—are an exception, but those studies are really more about parents (and parenting) than they are about children. In fact, studies have shown that children usually prefer their own invented toys to store-bought ones and don't always adhere to stereotypical expectations of gender-appropriate behavior (Chudacoff 2007:54–55). The trick is to find toys' meanings that were attributed by children, which might not accord with the well-meaning intentions of parents. Laurie Wilkie has speculated that five dolls' heads found in a garbage pit associated with a four-person household in Santa Monica, California, formed an angry older sister's response to the birth of a new baby. The two porcelain and three bisque doll's heads did not have their limbs, surely an expression of a violent emotion in reaction to a child's real-life experience (Wilkie 2000:103–104).

Home Away from Home

The archaeological record suggests that children found places to express themselves out of sight of adult supervision even when there was little room for privacy. Archaeological evidence has also been found that suggests men in the military sought privacy when they were away from home. At Raritan Landing in New Jersey we found a cache of artifacts—a brass buckle, an escutcheon plate, four brass gun parts, a brass ram pipe, a brass rammer, two brass trigger guards, at least seven gun parts, and a musket ball—hidden in a shovel-shaped slot that had been cut into the shale bedrock beneath the front floor of a house where British officers cantoned (were temporarily quartered) during the winter of 1777 (Figure 6.4). A silver-coated button marked "35" set inside a decorative swag and probably belonging to an officer was also found on the site, but there were buttons from other regiments too, some fancy and some not. A similar cache of artifacts—musket balls, gun flints, broken knives, forks, spoons, wine bottles, and fragments of butchered bone—was found by David Starbuck and his team under the compressed-dirt floor of a hut on Rogers Island in New York State (Starbuck 1999:61). In this case, the deposit dated to the French and Indian War and was associated with Rogers' Rangers, for whom

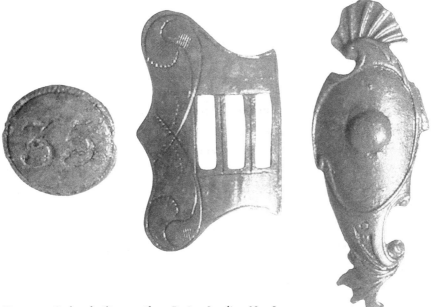

Figure 6.4. Cache of military artifacts, Raritan Landing, New Jersey.
Courtesy of John Milner Associates (Commonwealth Heritage Group).

the island was the principal base camp between 1757 and 1759. The hiding of possessions may be one way that people cope with intense communal living situations where privacy is rare and belongings are shared.

While the lives of homeless people would seem the least private of all possibilities and depressingly anonymous, archaeological studies have found evidence that even homeless people manage to conceal some personal possessions. An archaeological project in Indianapolis including a pedestrian survey of approximately one square mile identified three different site types—route sites, short-term sites, and campsites (Zimmerman and Welch 2011:73–77). "A commonly observed practice in campsites was caching behavior, that is, an effort to store some materials and to keep them protected from the elements or out of the hands of others until they could be retrieved at a later date" (Zimmerman and Welch 2011:75). The archaeologists did not open the caches, which were usually stowed either in black plastic garbage bags or in cardboard boxes stuffed into areas "difficult to access," but were told that they contained "family items or heirlooms, medications, books, favorite items of clothing, and a variety of other items difficult to carry around while the owner is away from camp" (2011:77). It would seem that no matter what the circumstances, people incorporate meaningful "stuff" into their lives.

We risk constructing an incomplete picture of past lives and culture if we leave out children, and it would also be a mistake to leave out the stories of clandestine activities that are so often crucial to adults' sense of well-being. In this chapter we have looked at the private activities that people do and the objects they use to allay their fears or communicate secretly in a way that will be understood by some and leave out others. In the case of children, clandestine activities in private (special) places are for figuring out how to live in the world they don't know yet. In the case of adults, their clandestine pursuits are for figuring out how to face the world they do know, with all its threats and dangers. In private they can admit vulnerability and do things to calm their fears. They can also express alternative identities, acting with personal agency in places where agency has been denied.

7

Selling Sex and Keeping Secrets

Agency is crucial in the past because it is significant in the present.
But the past has never been just about the past; it has always been what
makes the present able to live with itself.

(MOORE 2000:261)

We say we study archaeology to understand the past and its relation to the present. We also say that appreciating differences in the past will enable us to envision differences in the future. What is perhaps most instructive and reassuring about the archaeological evidence presented in this book is the proof of human agency. Agency in all sorts of situations—in private where people feel vulnerable and use rituals to make themselves feel safe, in situations of oppression where people continue cultural practices that make them feel "at home," in work situations where alienation inspires resistance, and in confined circumstances where acts of daring seem totally worth the risk. Pirates and smugglers are heroes in this context, but the real heroes are the participants in the Underground Railroad, both the conductors and the escapees, for whom the risks were enormous.

Not all acts of agency involve as much courage as did participation in the Underground Railroad, but most of them, even the criminal ones, demonstrate creativity. So much of historical archaeology—and so much of American life—deals with conformity that evidence for nonconformity is irresistibly fascinating. Acting as responsible scientists, we suspend moral judgment: the physical evidence of cartways built to illegally smuggle goods from one place to another excites us, and we love finding escape tunnels behind prison walls, and caches of alcohol bottles on worksites where drinking was forbidden. We also suspend disbelief. Bundles of trinkets hidden in vulnerable places are presented as rational, at least in culturally meaningful contexts. Folded coins made dairies safe and successful; bottles with pins and urine in them made people sick.

The evidence for prostitution in the past, however, is different. It is harder to suspend judgment. Maybe it is because we speak as women, or maybe it is because prostitution in the present does not seem so different from prostitution in the past. It is also special because it has never really been clandestine, although it has been treated with a blind eye, sometimes morally and legally condemned, and sometimes simply accepted as a necessary evil.

Prostitution as a Special Case

We have presented prostitution in the context of a broader discussion of agency as it pertains to going against society's norms, but prostitution is a special case and one that some have argued doesn't involve any agency at all. In her book *Paid For* (2013), Rachel Moran, a former prostitute in Ireland, claims that "those with the power and personal agency to do so would not choose prostitution as a way of life" (Moran 2013:224). Prostitutes do not have agency, she says, because it is their economic circumstances that force them into the profession. While Moran's experience as a prostitute took place in the 1990s, it is immediately relevant to a debate going on in the present, and we think that debate echoes many issues from the past. The debate is over whether or not prostitution should be decriminalized. Among others, Rachel Moran and the feminist icon Gloria Steinem are against decriminalization; Amnesty International, the World Health Organization, and a number of other health-related organizations (for example, Human Rights Watch, UNAIDS, the Global Commission on HIV and the Law, and the Open Society Foundations) are for it. An article published in the Sunday *New York Times Magazine* in the spring of 2016 (Bazelon 2016) took on this controversy, and the arguments presented in the article seem worth reviewing here. The overriding point in favor of decriminalization is that it would protect "the human rights of sex workers."

Amnesty International's draft policy statement, first developed in 2015 and published on May 26, 2016, calls for the review and repeal of laws that make sex workers vulnerable to human rights violations. The policy also points to the relationship between various kinds of discrimination (economic, gender, racial) that may lead people to turn to "sex work" to make a living. In place of treating prostitutes as criminals, the policy emphasizes states' obligation to ensure that they "are protected from exploitation and can use criminal law to address acts of exploitation." It urges states "to take appropriate measures to realize the economic, social, and cultural rights of all people so that no person enters sex work against their will or is compelled to rely on it as their only means of survival." A single point, tenth on the list, recognizes and respects "the agency of sex workers to articulate their own experiences and define the most appropriate solutions to ensure their own welfare and safety while also complying with broader, relevant international human rights principles" (Amnesty International 2016).

Amnesty International is not the first organization to argue for decriminalization. In the early 1970s, a group of prostitutes started an organization called COYOTE (Call Off Your Old Tired Ethics). They proposed decriminalization as a "feminist act" and saw themselves as "subverters of patriarchy, not as victims." They called themselves "sex workers" and saw their work as legitimate labor, no better or worse than other forms of paid labor. According to Bazelon, sex workers continue to want to change how they are perceived and policed. "They are fighting the legal status quo, social mores, and also mainstream feminism, which has typically focused on saving women from the sex trade rather than on supporting sex workers who demand greater rights" (Bazelon 2016:36). Some sex workers think decriminalization would make it safer and healthier. They envision a world "where women do it voluntarily in a way that is safe. If they are raped by a police officer or a client, they can lay a charge and know it will be investigated. Their kid won't be expelled from school and their landlord won't kick them out" (Bazelon 2016:38). Sex workers who favor decriminalization do not believe that prostitution is "inherently immoral or demeaning," and they do not think that criminal law should be used as an instrument of punishment or shame. To a great extent, Amnesty International and other organizational support of decriminalization agree, but their major emphasis is on health. The main stimulus for support of decriminalization of prostitution in the present has more to do with stemming the course of the HIV epidemic by increasing access to condoms and medical treatment than with protecting prostitutes' rights. In fact, COYOTE has accused other decriminalizers of caring more about the general health of society than about the women involved.

Speaking for the faction against decriminalization, Rachel Moran, whose book *Paid For* (2013) attracted a good deal of public attention when it was published, argues that the trade "preys on women already marginalized by class and race" and legalization would "calcify into law men's entitlement to buy sex" (Moran 2015:19). She does not dignify the practice or her own participation in it as "sex work," saying, "Selling my body wasn't a livelihood. There was no resemblance to ordinary employment in the ritual degradation of strangers using my body to satiate their urges." She was 15 when she entered the trade on the streets of Dublin and 22 when she escaped. The people who share Moran's view call themselves abolitionists, with an intended reference to the abolition of slavery. "If women are sex toys you can buy," one abolitionist has written, "think about the relationship between men and women, in marriage and otherwise" (Bazelon 2016:38). Abolitionists are not condemning the morality of the women who sell sex; they are condemning the morality of the men who buy it, and the societal mores that allow it. They tried in 1998 to convince the Clinton administration to define all prostitution as trafficking and thus expand and stiffen criminal punishment, but their efforts failed. Taking a different tack with the Bush administration, abolitionists formed a coalition with faith-based groups, which managed to rescue women and girls abroad but in many instances abused women in the process (Bazelon 2016:39).

This controversy, it turns out, is not new. In her book about Progressive Era prostitution in America, Ruth Rosen (1982) describes reform efforts begun in the 1870s as falling into two categories. One, the "regulationists," believed that "prostitution, though evil, was necessary to accommodate men and preserve the purity of the home" (Rosen 1982:9). They characterized prostitutes as "autonomous" working women who were "free of moralistic sexual control and thus beyond the control of patriarchy" (Roberts 1992:246). They thought prostitution was ineradicable and that consequently, state regulation was the only practical means of controlling the social and medical problems that it presented. Like the decriminalizers of today, their biggest concern was not the degradation or economic disadvantage of women in the profession, but the spread of disease. They wanted to institute compulsory medical examinations of all prostitutes and compulsory hospitalization of those with venereal disease (Rosen 1982:9). Their approach was based on an interpretation of the available scientific and medical evidence, and they looked to the law and social control for solutions.

Another group of reformers in the 1870s, known variously as "social purity" advocates, abolitionists, or "antireglementarians," were for abolishing prostitution altogether through the reformation of the nation's morals. In addition to the abolition of prostitution, they were for censoring pornography, introducing sex education, prosecuting prostitutes' customers, and establishing women's right to refuse to have marital sex (Rosen 1982:11). Although seemingly more moralistic than today's abolitionists, they, or at least the feminist members of this group, were more sympathetic to prostitutes' plight in the socioeconomic system than the "regulationists." They "condemned male sexual conduct and expressed feelings of identification with prostitutes," some of them comparing it to the "perfectly respectable mantle of marriage" (Rosen 1982:11–12). The major aim of the nineteenth-century abolitionists, however, was to "impose a single standard of chastity on both sexes" which, Rosen argues, "diverted public attention from the pressing economic and social problems of rapid growth and urbanization" (1982:260).

It appears that neither attitudes toward nor cures for prostitution have ever been straightforward. As we said in the first chapter of this book, however, the subject always attracts interest. Among all the things Rachel Moran says prostitution is—violence against women, a degrading and exploitative exchange, sexual humiliation, sexual slavery, misuse of male power—she thinks it may be "precisely because the act of prostituting oneself is so inherently alien to humans that people are fascinated by it" (Moran 2013:194). Perhaps. Bazelon's article in the *New York Times Magazine* was ostensibly written to discuss decriminalization as a feminist issue. Notwithstanding its rigor, the article is heavily illustrated with eight portraits of real-life prostitutes, four of the photos covering a full page. In addition, the cover of the magazine is illustrated with three rows of prostitutes, totaling 36 individuals, 3 of them identifiably male. The males may be pimps rather than prostitutes. The pictures are not particularly sexy, but they are photographs of real people. Is the fascination, as Moran speculates, because they do something alien? Is it that they have agency to defy societal norms? Is it more than just sex? It seems somewhat inappropriate that the *New York Times Magazine* would use "sex to sell the product," but maybe they meant to dignify the practitioners. That surely is what archaeology has tried to do up to this time.

We have treated prostitution as a gender issue. It falls within the study of women's work. The women who did it in the nineteenth century did it because there were few alternatives. Paid labor was so underpaid that it didn't provide women, especially women who did not have the support of a man, enough of an income to survive, and certainly not enough to participate in the consumer society that was burgeoning around them. Prostitutes in the nineteenth century came mainly from the working class; they were often initiated into sex early in their lives within their own communities and did not have prudish values about using it to make much-needed money. There is no basis to believe, however, that the sex itself was any less demeaning or dehumanizing than the sex reported by Rachel Moran or the Rios women interviewed by Oscar Lewis. The historian Ruth Rosen puts it well, and it seems worth quoting her at length:

> I regard prostitution neither as the worst form of exploitation women have ever suffered, nor as a noble or liberating occupation, but rather as a dangerous and degrading occupation that, given the limited and unattractive alternatives, has enabled thousands of women to escape even worse danger and deprivation. When I look closely at the life stories of poor women during the early years of this century, I am struck again and again by most prostitutes' view of their work as "easier" and less oppressive than other survival strategies they might have chosen. The statement that prostitution offered certain opportunities and advantages for some women, however, should not be interpreted as a positive or romanticized assessment of the life of a prostitute. Instead, it should be read as an indictment of the limited range of opportunities that early twentieth-century women faced in their daily struggle for economic, social, and psychological well being. Denied access to social and economic power because of their gender and class status, poor women made their choices from a position of socially structured powerlessness. (Rosen 1982:xvii)

Passing Judgment

A long time ago, the anthropologist Robert Redfield confronted the issue of making value judgments in the context of tracing the transformation of society from simplicity to complexity. In *The Primitive World and Its Transformations* (1953:131) he tells the unforgettable story of Petalesharoo, the Pawnee son of a chief, who stopped the yearly sacrifice of a young girl from another tribe, saying it was his father's wish to abolish this sacrifice and offering himself in her stead. Redfield cannot help but admire the courage of Petalesharoo to act "against the moral order of his own group." In the context of discussing what an anthropologist is and is not supposed to feel, Redfield admits to being distressed by the Siriono of the Bolivian forest, who leave their aging kinsmen behind "without a word," while at the same time he admires the Yagua for respecting "even a child's desire to be alone by refraining from speaking to him when he turns his face to the wall" (1953:140). While it has been more than a half-century since Redfield wrestled with these issues, they are, at least to an extent, still with us.

It is difficult for us, that is, the female authors of this book, to talk about prostitution without passing judgment, not on the women who have had to sell sex to make ends meet, but on the social systems that make sex a salable commodity. Perhaps prostitutes in the past were no more alienated from their work than factory laborers. Perhaps the commodification of sex in the nineteenth century was qualitatively different than the commodification today, but it is not an issue that has gone away. We are not for decriminalization. We do not think it is acceptable or desirable to accept violence against women in any form for any purpose. If we have learned anything from the past about this particular institution, it is that it wasn't good for women in the past, and it isn't good for them in the present.

Rachel Moran's study (2013) based on her own experience makes it eminently clear how psychologically damaging it is to sell one's body (one's self), an assessment echoed by Daniel Steele, who concluded that the work erodes the soul (2017:245). There is no reason to believe that it was any less damaging in the past. Moran describes in excruciating detail how necessary it is for a prostitute to disassociate herself from what she is doing, how much denial it takes to bear the sexual revulsion that is a daily experience, and to endure the shame that comes with sexual abuse. Like other workers, prostitutes are alienated from themselves, but in their case, according to Moran, there is nothing left. Archaeologists, of course, cannot read that kind of psychological damage from the material remains found on nineteenth-century brothel sites, but we do have evidence that prostitutes in northeastern brothels, at least, were exploited as workers. They were treated one way when they were working (fancy foods, luxurious clothes and accoutrements) and another when they were not. They suffered from venereal disease and spent energy and ingenuity treating it and preventing pregnancy. The presence of full-term natal remains in the Five Points privy suggests that some prostitutes may even have been driven to committing infanticide.

In the frontier West, prostitutes found opportunities for independence and entrepreneurship, especially in the early stages of settlement, during the boom phases. Women's work was in demand in the overwhelmingly male populations. However, any young woman who went West to a mining camp hoping for wage labor in conventional domestic services might not have been too surprised by what she needed to do to survive. In the East, a woman in domestic service—or even government service—often experienced demands for sexual services if she wanted to keep her job (Ames 1875:374; Ellis 1869:386; Rosen 1982:149, 151, 161). In the West some enterprising women found independence and economic opportunity working as prostitutes or operating brothels, especially before mining was industrialized and camps developed into towns with a full complement of social institutions—including families.

When boom turned to bust, women with resources moved on; those without were left destitute. However, when a woman in the West was far from family and her own past, she probably had a fair chance of creating a new persona, starting a new life, and finding a life partner. Chinese prostitutes rarely experienced independence and opportunity. Most Chinese women brought to the West had been tricked, bought, betrayed, enslaved, or indentured. There was a large market for their services and little chance of moving from prostitute to wife: Chinese men did not plan to stay, and a Chinese woman could not legally marry a Euro-American man.

We realize that it may seem hypocritical to reserve judgment on the acts of agency, other than prostitution, discussed in this book. We appear to celebrate pirates' agency, rather than condemning them as criminals, even though we know that in our own time, Somalian pirates, to name just one group, have committed crimes we cannot condone. We are fascinated by the archaeological evidence for prison escapes, although we surely don't want escaped prisoners in our own backyards; and we admire workers who undermine their bosses on the job, as long as our employees don't undermine us. We carefully avoid questioning the efficacy of magical practices that objectively don't work, and we reserve judgment on customs that are intended to cause harm to other human beings. Clearly, we have been selective in our judgments, but we can't help ourselves. Prostitution is too close to our experience as women to discuss at a distance.

Conclusion

Agency is notoriously difficult to measure, or even identify. It is "entangled," as Ian Hodder would say, with everything else. "Humans manipulate things in order to resist domination, transform meanings, undermine authority and power, create identities, and sustain notions of personhood" (Hodder

2012:215). Examples of all of these have been described here. How much agency is constrained by society's structures, whether they be in the environment, the economy, the social structure, or the culture, is a question that has been debated for a long time (McGuire 1992:118). It would seem, however, that in both small ways and big ways, Americans in the eighteenth and nineteenth centuries found ways to defy the norms. The material evidence for keeping secrets and selling sex reveals people using their ingenuity to confront power in a variety of ways. They broke the law, escaped from bondage, created dual identities, defied work regimens, and found innumerable unconventional paths to making money. While clandestine activities and prostitution are not exactly the same thing, they share the human capacity to act outside convention.

Archaeology has special access to defiant behavior. We find things that are both intentionally and unintentionally hidden. What's wrong with this picture? That is a useful question to pose when interpreting any archaeological site. It has proved essential to finding archaeological brothel sites. Anomaly leads to places that predictable findings do not. In Washington, DC, off-the-charts-expensive tablewares in an undesirable neighborhood led us to look over the wall to the biggest brothel in the city during the Civil War.

Beginning with the things, we get to discover what was not meant to be discovered. We cannot recommend a plan for future research in this area, because the whole point is that we don't know what is still hidden and yet to be found. What we can recommend is keeping an eye out for what doesn't fit, what doesn't immediately make sense, because it is those things that might lead to people who acted independently. Evidence for creativity in the past, for agency, is especially gratifying because it reassures us that there is such a thing. We are not just pawns of our society. While we may never figure out whether agency is influenced more by society's constraints or by human independent actions, the interplay between them, as interpreted from archaeological finds, provides a fascinating framework for dissecting the past.

References Cited

Alexander, Priscilla

1998   Prostitution: Still a Difficult Issue for Feminists. In *Sex Work: Writings by Women in the Sex Industry*, edited by Frederique Delacoste and Priscilla Alexander, pp. 184–230. Cleis Press, San Francisco.

Allen, June

1976   *Dolly's House*. Tongass, Ketchikan, Alaska.

Ames, Mary Clemmer

1875   Ten Years in Washington: Life and Scenes in the National Capital, as a Woman Sees Them. A. D. Worthington, Hartford, Connecticut.

Amnesty International

2016   Policy Statement on State Obligations to Respect, Protect, and Fulfill the Human Rights of Sex Workers. https://www.amnesty.org/download/Documents/POL3040622016ENGLISH.PDF.

Armstrong, Douglas V., and LuAnn Wurst

2003   Clay Faces in an Abolitionist Church: The Wesleyan Methodist Church in Syracuse, New York. *Historical Archaeology* 37(2):19–37.

Asbury, Herbert

1928   *The Gangs of New York. An Informal History of the Underworld*. Garden City Publishing, Garden City, New York.

Baker, Steven G.

1972   A Prospectus of Continuing Research on the Goldbelt Theatre and Social History of the Vanoli Properties in Ouray, Colorado. Institute of Archeology and Anthropology, University of South Carolina, Columbia.

Barbour, Hugh, and J. William Frost

1988   *The Quakers*. Friends United Press, Richmond, Indiana.

Bard, James C., and Robert M. Weaver

2014   Chapter 7. Medicinal Assemblages. In *The Other Side of Sandpoint: Early History and Archaeology beside the Tracks*. The Sandpoint Archaeology Project 2006–2013. Vol. 2: *Material Culture of Everyday Life*, edited by Mark S. Warner. SWCA Report No. 14-48. Prepared for Idaho Transportation Department, District 1, Coeur d'Alene, Idaho. SWCA Environmental Consultants, Portland, Oregon.

Barton, Christopher P., and David G. Orr

2015   A Practice Theory of Improvisation at the African American Community of Timbuctoo, Burlington County, New Jersey. In *The Archaeology of Race in the Northeast*, edited by Christopher N. Matthews and Allison Manfra McGovern, pp. 198–211. University Press of Florida, Gainesville.

Battle-Baptiste, Whitney

2010   "Sweepin' Spirits: Power and Transformation on the Plantation Landscape." In *The Archaeology and Preservation of Gendered Landscapes*, edited by Sherene Baugher and Suzanne Spencer-Wood, pp. 81–94. Springer, New York.

2011   *Black Feminist Archaeology*. Left Coast Press, Walnut Creek, California.

Baxter, Jane Eva

2005a   Making Space for Children in Archaeology. Interpretations. In *Children in Action: Perspectives in the Archaeology of Childhood*, edited by Jane Eva Baxter. Archaeological Papers of the American Anthropological Association, No. 1. John Wiley and Sons, Malden, Massachusetts.

2005b   *The Archaeology of Childhood, Children, Gender, and Material Culture*. Altamira Press, Walnut Creek, California.

Bazelon, Emily

2016   Oppression or Profession? *New York Times Magazine*, May 8, pp. 36–43 and 56–57.

Beaudry, Mary C.

1989   The Lowell Boott Mills Complex and Its Housing: Material Expressions of Corporate Ideology. *Historical Archaeology* 23(1):19–32.

1992   Public Aesthetics versus Personal Experience: Worker Health and Well-Being in Nineteenth-Century Lowell, Massachusetts. *Historical Archaeology* 27(2):90–105.

Beaudry, Mary C., Lauren J. Cook, and Stephen A. Mrozowski

1991   Artifacts and Active Voices: Material Culture as Social Discourse. In *The Archaeology of Inequality*, edited by Randall H. McGuire and Robert Paynter, pp. 150–191. Basil Blackwell, Oxford.

Bellocq, E. J.

1976   *Photographs from Storyville, the Red Light District of New Orleans*. Reproduced from prints made by Lee Friedlander. Random House, New York.

Blackmar, Elizabeth

1989   *Manhattan for Rent, 1785–1850*. Cornell University Press, Ithaca.

Blair, Madeleine

1986   *Madeleine: An Autobiography*. Reprinted. Persea Books, New York. Originally published 1919.

Blakey, Michael L., and Lesley M. Rankin-Hill

2009   The Skeletal Biology of the New York African Burial Ground, Part I. *The New York African Burial Ground, Unearthing the African Presence in Colonial New York*, Vol. 1. Howard University Press, Washington, DC.

Blee, Catherine Holder
1991   Sorting Functionally Mixed Artifact Assemblages with Multiple Regression: A Comparative Study in Historical Archaeology. Doctoral dissertation, Department of Anthropology, University of Colorado, Boulder. University Microfilms, Ann Arbor.

Bonasera, Michael C.
2000   Good for What Ails You: Medicinal Practices at Five Points. In *Tales of Five Points: Working Class in Nineteenth-Century New York*, Vol. II, edited by Rebecca Yamin, pp. 371–419. Prepared for Edwards and Kelcy Engineers, Inc. and General Services Administration, Region 2. John Milner Associates, Inc. (now Commonwealth Heritage Group, Inc.), 535 North Church Street, West Chester, Pennsylvania.

Bond, Kathleen H.
1989   Company Policy and Alcohol Use at the Boott Mills Housing, Lowell, Massachusetts. Paper presented at the Annual Meeting of the Society for Historical Archaeology, Baltimore, Maryland.

Boschke, A.
1861   *Topographical Map of the District of Columbia Surveyed in the Years 1856, '57, '58, and '59*. Drawn by A. Boschke. Engraved by D. McClelland, Washington, DC. McClelland, Blanchard, and Mohun. Map on file. Geography and Map Division, Library of Congress, Washington, DC.

Bourdieu, Pierre
1972   *Outline of a Theory of Practice*. Cambridge Studies in Social Anthropology. Cambridge University Press, New York.

Boyd, Andrew
1867   *Boyd's Washington and Georgetown Directory*. Andrew Boyd, Washington, DC.
1868   *Boyd's Washington and Georgetown Directory*. Andrew Boyd, Washington, DC.
1872   *Boyd's Washington and Georgetown Directory*. Andrew Boyd, Washington, DC.

Boyd, William H.
1878   *Boyd's Directory of the District of Columbia*. William H. Boyd, Washington, DC.
1879   *Boyd's Directory of the District of Columbia*, William H. Boyd, Washington, DC.
1881   *Boyd's Directory of the District of Columbia*. William H. Boyd, Washington, DC.
1882   *Boyd's Directory of the District of Columbia*. William H. Boyd, Washington, DC.
1885   *Boyd's Directory of the District of Columbia*. William H. Boyd, Washington, DC.

Brighton, Stephen A.
2000   The Evolution of Ceramic Production and Distribution as Viewed from Five Points. Appendix B in *Tales of Five Points: Working-Class Life in Nineteenth-Century New York*. Vol. I: *A Narrative History and Archeology of Block 160*, edited by Rebecca Yamin, pp. B-1–B-42. Prepared for Edwards and Kelcy Engineers, Inc. and General Services Administration, Region 2. John Milner Associates, Inc. (now Commonwealth Heritage Group, Inc.), 535 North Church Street, West Chester, Pennsylvania.

2008   Degrees of Alienation: The Material Evidence of the Irish and Irish American Experience, 1850–1910. *Historical Archaeology* 42(4):132–153.

Brodie, Janet F.

1994   *Contraception and Abortion in Nineteenth-Century America*. Cornell University Press, Ithaca.

Buel, James William

1883   *Mysteries and Miseries of America's Great Cities, Embracing New York, Washington City, San Francisco, Salt Lake City, and New Orleans*. Historical Publishing, St. Louis.

Buntline, Ned

1848   *The Mysteries and Miseries of New York: A Story of Real Life*. Part I. Wright American Fiction, Vol. 1, 1774–1850, number 1527. Place of publication not identified.

Burnston, Sharon Ann

1982   Babies in the Well: An Underground Insight into Deviant Behavior in Eighteenth-Century Philadelphia. *Pennsylvania Magazine of History and Biography*, 147–185. Berford, New York.

Burrow, Ian, William B. Liebeknecht, Patrick Harshbarger, and Alison Haley

2014   Reedy Island Cart Road Site 4 [7NC-F-153], U.S. Route 301 Project, St. Georges Hundred, New Castle County, Delaware, Phase II Archaeological Investigation and Alternative Mitigation. A Research Program to Test the Cart Road Predictive Model through Geophysical Survey, Lidar Image Analysis, Soil Compaction Studies, Topographic Mapping, and Archeological Excavation. Prepared for Delaware Department of Transportation, Dover, Delaware. Hunter Research Inc.

Bush, David R.

2009   Maintaining or Mixing Southern Culture in a Northern Prison: Johnson's Island Military Prison. In *The Archaeology of Institutional Life,* edited by April M. Beisaw and James G. Gibb, pp. 154–171. University of Alabama Press, Tuscaloosa.

Butler, Judith

1999   *Gender Trouble, Feminism and the Subversion of Identity*. Routledge, New York.

Califia, Pat

1994   *Public Sex: The Culture of Radical Sex*. Cleis Press, Pittsburgh.

Calvert, Karin

1992   *Children in the House: The Material Culture of Childhood in America, 1600–1900*. Northeastern University Press, Boston.

Cantwell, Anne-Marie, and Diana diZerega Wall

2001   *Unearthing Gotham: The Archaeology of New York City*. Yale University Press, New Haven.

Cheek, Charles D., and Donna J. Seifert

1994   Neighborhoods and Household Types in Nineteenth-Century Washington, D.C.: Fannie Hill and Mary McNamara in Hooker's Division. In *Historical Archaeology of the Chesapeake*, edited by Paul A. Shackel and Barbara J. Little, pp. 267–282. Smithsonian Institution Press, Washington, DC.

Cheek, Charles D., Donna J. Seifert, Patrick W. O'Bannon, Cheryl A. Holt, B. R. Roulette, Jr., Joseph Balicki, Glenn G. Ceponis, and Dana B. Heck

1991   Phase II and Phase III Archaeological Investigations at the Site of the Proposed International Cultural and Trade Center/Federal Office Complex, Federal Triangle, Washington, DC. Report to the Pennsylvania Avenue Development Corporation, Washington, DC, from John Milner Associates, Inc., Alexandria, Virginia.

Chudacoff, Howard P.

2007   *Children at Play: An American History*. New York University Press, New York.

Cofield, Sarah Rivers

2014   Keeping a Crooked Sixpence: Coin Magic and Religion in the Colonial Chesapeake. *Historical Archaeology* 48(3): 84–105.

Commissioners of the District of Columbia (CDC)

1914   *Acts of Congress Affecting the District of Columbia*. Commissioners of the District of Columbia, Washington, DC.

Conkey, Margaret W., and Joan M. Gero

1991   Tensions, Pluralities, and Engendering Archaeology: An Introduction to Women and Prehistory. In *Engendering Archaeology, Women and Prehistory*, edited by Joan M. Gero and Margaret W. Conkey, pp. 3–30. Blackwell, Oxford.

Connelly, Mark Thomas

1984   Prostitution, Venereal Disease and American Medicine. In *Women and Health in America*, edited by Judith Walzer, pp. 196–221. Originally published 1980. University of Wisconsin Press, Madison.

Costello, Jessica

2014   Tracing the Footsteps of Ritual: Concealed Footwear in America. *Historical Archaeology* 48(3):35–51.

Costello, Julia G.

2000   Redlight Voices: An Archaeological Drama of Late Nineteenth-Century Prostitution. In *Archaeologies of Sexuality*, edited by Robert A. Schmidt and Barbara A. Voss, pp. 160–175. Routledge, London.

Crist, Thomas A.

2005   Babies in the Privy: Prostitution, Infanticide, and Abortion in New York City's Five Points District. *Historical Archaeology* 39(1):19–46.

Davidson, James M.

2004   Rituals Captured in Context and Time: Charm Use in North Dallas Freedman's Town (1869–1907), Dallas, Texas. *Historical Archaeology* 38(2):22–54.

Dawdy, Shannon Lee, and Richard Weybring

2008   Beneath the Rising Sun: "Frenchness" and the Archaeology of Desire. *International Journal of Historical Archaeology* 12(4):370–387.

Deagan, Kathleen

2007   Eliciting Contraband through Archaeology: Illicit Trade in Eighteenth-Century St. Augustine. *Historical Archaeology* 41(4):98–116.

DeCunzo, LuAnn

1995   Reform, Respite, Ritual: An Archaeology of Institutions: The Magdalen Society of Philadelphia, 1800–1850. *Historical Archaeology* 29(3):1–164.

Delacoste, Frederique, and Priscilla Alexander (editors)

1998   *Sex Work: Writings by Women in the Sex Industry*. Cleis Press, San Francisco.

Delle, James A., and Mary Ann Levine

2004   Excavations at the Thaddeus Stevens and Lydia Hamilton Smith Site, Lancaster, Pennsylvania: Archaeological Evidence for the Underground Railroad? *Northeast Historical Archaeology* 33:131–152.

Delle, James A., and Jason Shellenhamer

2008   Archaeology at the Parvin Homestead: Searching for the Material Legacy of the Underground Railroad. *Historical Archaeology* 42(2):38–62.

District of Columbia Building Permits (DCBP)

1877–1926   District of Columbia Building Permits, 1877–1926. Microfilm. National Archives and Records Administration, Washington, DC.

District of Columbia General Assessments (DCGA)

1829–1887   District of Columbia General Assessments. National Archives and Records Administration, Washington, DC.

1886–1934   District of Columbia General Assessments. Microfilm. Washingtoniana Room, Martin Luther King, Jr., Branch, District of Columbia Public Library, Washington, DC.

District of Columbia Supreme Court (DCSC)

1886   Papers Relating to the Estate of Mary Ann Hall. District of Columbia Archives, Washington, DC.

District of Columbia Tax Books (DCTB)

1840–1879   District of Columbia Tax Books. National Archives and Records Administration, Washington, DC.

Dobres, Marcia-Anne, and John Robb (editors)

2000   *Agency in Archaeology*. Routledge, London.

Eichner, Katrina

2014   Female Injectors: Vaginal Syringes—Their Use at the Padelford Privy. Paper presented at the Annual Meeting of the Society for Historical Archaeology, Quebec City.

Ellis, John B.

1869   *The Sights and Secrets of the National Capital*. United States Publishing, New York.

Emerson, Matthew C.

1999   African Inspirations in a New World Art and Artifact: Decorated Tobacco Pipes from the Chesapeake. In *"I, Too, Am America": Archaeological Studies of African-*

American Life, edited by Theresa A. Singleton, pp. 47–82. University Press of Virginia, Charlottesville.

Evening Star

1862–1873   *Evening Star*. Microfilm. Washingtoniana Division, Martin Luther King, Jr., Branch, District of Columbia Public Library, Washington, DC.

Ewen, Charles R.

2006   Introduction to *X Marks the Spot: The Archaeology of Piracy*, edited by Russell K. Skowronek and Charles R. Ewen, pp. 1–12. New Perspectives on Maritime History and Nautical Archaeology, University Press of Florida, Gainesville.

Fellows, Kristen

2016   Homosocial Bonding in the Brothel: Analyzing Space and Material Culture through Documents. Paper presented at the Annual Meeting of the Society for Historical Archaeology, Washington, DC.

Fennell, Christopher C., and M. Chris Manning (editors)

2014   Manifestations of Magic: The Archaeology and Material Culture of Folk Religion. *Historical Archaeology* 48(3).

Ferguson, Leland G.

1999   "The Cross Is a Magic Sign": Marks on Eighteenth-Century Bowls from South Carolina. In *"I, Too, Am America": Archaeological Studies of African-American Life*, edited by Theresa A. Singleton, pp. 116–131. University Press of Virginia, Charlottesville.

Fitts, Robert K.

1999   The Archaeology of Middle-Class Domesticity and Gentility in Victorian Brooklyn. *Historical Archaeology* 33(1):39–62.

Foster, George G.

1990[1850]   *New York by Gas-Light and Other Urban Sketches*. Edited and with an introduction by Stuart Blumin. University of California Press, Berkeley.

Foster, Michael S., John M. Lindly, and Ronald F. Ryden

2004   Celestials and Soiled Doves: The Archaeology and History of Lots 4–9, Block 13 of Historic Prescott's Original Townsite: The Prescott City Center Project. *SWCA Cultural Resource Report* No. 03–386. Phoenix.

Gardner, Andrew

2007   Introduction: Social Agency, Power, and Being Human. In *Agency Uncovered: Archaeological Perspectives on Social Agency, Power, and Being Human*, edited by Andrew Gardner, pp. 1–15. Left Coast Press, Walnut Creek, California.

Garman, James C.

2005   *Detention Castles of Stone and Steel: Landscape, Labor, and the Urban Penitentiary*. University of Tennessee Press, Knoxville.

Geiger, Lisa

2013   Consumer Hygiene and Reproductive Healthcare: The Female Body in Early America. Draft copy of article provided to R. Yamin for review.

Gerhardt, Juliette

2016   "Living through the American Revolution," with Rebecca Yamin. In *Archaeology of the City—The Museum of the American Revolution Site, Philadelphia, PA*, edited by Rebecca Yamin, pp. 68–88. Report prepared for the Museum of the American Revolution, Commonwealth Heritage Group, West Chester, PA.

Gero, Joan M., and Margaret W. Conkey 1991   *Engendering Archaeology: Women and Prehistory*. Blackwell, Oxford, UK.

Giddens, Anthony

1995   *A Contemporary Critique of Historical Materialism*. Stanford University Press, Stanford, California.

Gilfoyle, Timothy J.

1992   *City of Eros, New York City, Prostitution and the Commercialization of Sex, 1790–1920*. W. W. Norton, New York.

Glassie, Henry

1988   Meaningful Things and Appropriate Myths: The Artifact's Place in American Studies. In *Material Life in America 1600–1860*, edited by Robert Blair St. George, pp. 63–92. Northeastern University Press, Boston.

Goldman, Marion

1981   *Gold Diggers and Silver Miners: Prostitution and Social Life on the Comstock Lode*. University of Michigan Press, Ann Arbor.

Grafton, John

1977   *New York in the Nineteenth Century, 321 Engravings from Harper's Weekly and Other Contemporary Sources*. Dover, New York.

Green, Constance McLaughlin

1962   *Washington: A History of the Capital, 1800–1950*. 2 vols. Princeton University Press, Princeton.

Griggs, Heather J.

2000   Competition and Economic Strategy in the Needle Trades in a Nineteenth-Century Working-Class Neighborhood. In *Tales of Five Points: Working-Class Life in Nineteenth-Century New York*, Vol. II, edited by Rebecca Yamin, pp. 288–304. Prepared for Edwards and Kelcy Engineers, Inc., and General Services Administration, Region 2. John Milner Associates, Inc. (now Commonwealth Heritage Group, Inc.), 535 North Church Street, West Chester, Pennsylvania.

Haller, John S., and Robin M. Haller

1974   *The Physician and Sexuality in Victorian America*. University of Illinois Press, Urbana.

Hamilton, Christopher E.

2006   The Pirate Ship *Whydah*. In *X Marks the Spot: The Archaeology of Piracy*, edited by Russell K. Skowronek and Charles R. Ewen, pp. 131–159. New Perspectives on Maritime History and Nautical Archaeology, University Press of Florida, Gainesville.

Hill, Marilyn Wood

1993   *Their Sisters' Keepers: Prostitution in New York City, 1830–1870.* University of California Press, Berkeley.

Hine, Darlene Clark

1989   Rape and the Inner Lives of Black Women in the Middle West. *Signs* 14(4):912–920.

Hodder, Ian

1999   *The Archaeological Process, an Introduction.* Blackwell, Oxford, UK.

2012   *Entangled: An Archaeology of the Relationships between Humans and Things.* Wiley-Blackwell, West Sussex, UK.

Hodgson, Barbara

2001   *In the Arms of Morpheus: The Tragic History of Laudanum, Morphine, and Patent Medicines.* Firefly Books, Buffalo, New York.

Holloway, Emory (editor)

1921   *The Uncollected Poetry and Prose of Walt Whitman.* Doubleday, Page, Garden City, New York.

Hopkins, Griffith M.

1887   *Real Estate Plat-Book of Washington, District of Columbia.* Griffith M. Hopkins, Philadelphia.

Ingle, Marjorie, Jean Howson, and Edward S. Rutsch

1990   A Stage 1A Cultural Resources Survey of the Proposed Foley Square Project, Manhattan, New York. Prepared by Historic Conservation and Interpretation, Inc., for Edwards and Kelcey Engineers, Inc. Manuscript on file, Landmarks Preservation Commission, New York.

Johnson, Amanda

2010   A Glimpse into the Lives of Boston's "Butterflies." An Analysis of the Artifacts Pertaining to Personification of Self from the 27/29 Endicott Street Privy. Thesis, independent work for distinction in archaeology, Boston University.

Johnson, Matthew

1999   *Archaeological Theory: An Introduction.* Blackwell, Oxford, UK.

2007   Agency, Structure and Archaeological Practice. In *Agency Uncovered: Archaeological Perspectives on Social Agency, Power, and Being Human,* edited by Andrew Gardner, pp. 241–247. Left Coast Press, Walnut Creek, California.

Johnston, Norman

1994   *Escapes from Eastern State Penitentiary.* Eastern State Penitentiary Historic Site, Philadelphia.

Jordan, Peter

2007   Examining the Role of Agency in Hunter-Gatherer Cultural Transmission. In *Agency Uncovered: Archaeological Perspectives on Social Agency, Power, and Being Human,* edited by Andrew Gardner, pp. 108–134. Left Coast Press, Walnut Creek, California.

Keim, Alexander D.

2016   Sex Workers in the City: Presentation and Interaction in 19th-Century Boston's Urban Landscape. Paper presented at the Annual Meeting of the Society for Historical Archaeology, Washington, DC.

Ketz, K. Anne, Elizabeth J. Abel, and Andrew J. Schmidt

2005   Public Images and Private Reality: An Analysis of Differentiation in a Nineteenth-Century St. Paul Bordello. *Historical Archaeology* 39(1):74–88.

King, Thomas F.

2005   *Doing Archaeology: A Cultural Resource Management Perspective.* Left Coast Press, Walnut Creek, California.

Kingsdale, John M.

1973   The "Poor Man's Club": Social Functions of the Urban Working-Class Saloon. *American Quarterly* 25(4):472–489.

Kinkor, Kenneth J.

2016   Artifacts That Talk Like Pirates: Jolly Roger Iconography and Archaeological Sites. In *Pieces of Eight: More Archaeology of Piracy*, edited by Charles R. Ewen and Russell K. Skowronek, pp. 228–238. New Perspectives on Maritime History and Nautical Archaeology, University Press of Florida, Gainesville.

Kisling, Breanna, and Mark S. Warner

2014   Chapter 13. From the "Bloom of Youth" to "Dye for the Whiskers": Grooming the Women and Men of Sandpoint. In *The Other Side of Sandpoint: Early History and Archaeology beside the Tracks*. The Sandpoint Archaeology Project 2006–2013. Vol. 2: *Material Culture of Everyday Life*, edited by Mark S. Warner. SWCA Report No. 14–48. Prepared for Idaho Transportation Department, District 1, Coeur d'Alene, Idaho. SWCA Environmental Consultants, Portland, Oregon.

Kohler, Timothy, and Eric Blinman

1985   Solving Mixture Problems in Archaeology: Analysis of Ceramic Materials for Dating and Demographic Reconstruction. *Journal of Anthropological Archaeology* 6(1):1–28.

Kooistra, AnneMarie

2016   The Enterprising Career of Tom Savage in Los Angeles' Red-Light District, 1870–1909. Paper presented at the 2016 Annual Meeting of the Society for Historical Archaeology, 6–9 January 2016, Washington, DC.

LaRoche, Cheryl Janifer

2014   *Free Black Communities and the Underground Railroad: The Geography of Resistance.* University of Illinois Press, Urbana.

Lee, Mabel Barbee

1968   *Back in Cripple Creek.* Doubleday, Garden City, New York.

Leech, Margaret

1941   *Reveille in Washington: 1860–1865.* Harper, New York.

Leone, Mark P.

2005   *The Archaeology of Liberty in an American Capital: Excavations in Annapolis.* University of California Press, Berkeley.

Lewis, Oscar

1965   *La Vida, A Puerto Rican Family in the Culture of Poverty—San Juan and New York.* Random House, New York.

Los Angeles, City of

1878   *Revised Charter and Compiled Ordinances and Resolutions of the City of Los Angeles.* Compiled and indexed by Wm. M. Caswell. Evening Express Printing Establishment, Los Angeles.

Loveyer, Free (editor)

1859   *Directory to the Seraglios in New York, Philadelphia, Boston, and All the Principal Cities in the Union.* In the archival collection of the New-York Historical Society.

Lowry, Thomas P.

1994   *The Story the Soldiers Wouldn't Tell: Sex in the Civil War.* Stackpole Books, Mechanicsville, Pennsylvania.

Lucas, Michael T.

2014   Empowered Objects: Material Expressions of Spiritual Beliefs in the Colonial Chesapeake Region. *Historical Archaeology* 48(3):106–124.

Luiz, Jade

2014   Under the Corset: Health, Hygiene, and Maternity in Boston's North End. Paper presented at the Annual Meeting of the Society of Historical Archaeology, Quebec City.

2016   Ghosts in the Archives: Using Archaeology to Return Life to Historical Prostitutes. Paper presented at the Annual Meeting of the Society for Historical Archaeology, Washington, DC.

Lusardi, Wayne R.

2006   The Beaufort Inlet Shipwreck Artifact Assemblage. In *X Marks the Spot: The Archaeology of Piracy*, edited by Russell K. Skowronek and Charles R. Ewen, pp. 196–218. University Press of Florida, Gainesville.

Manning, M. Chris

2014   The Material Culture of Ritual Concealments in the United States. *Historical Archaeology* 48(3):52–83.

2015   Histarch [list] post, 9 April 2015.

Martin, Edward Winslow [James D. McCabe, Jr.]

1868   *The Secrets of the Great City: A Work Descriptive of the Virtues and the Vices, the Mysteries, Miseries, and Crimes of New York City.* National Publishing, successors to Jones Brothers. Republished as *New York by Sunlight and Gaslight* by James D. McCabe, Jr., 1882.

Matthews, Christopher N., and Allison Manfra McGovern (editors)

2015   *The Archaeology of Race in the Northeast.* University of Florida Press, Gainesville.

Mayne, Alan

1993   *The Imagined Slum, Newspaper Representation in Three Cities, 1870–1914.* Leicester University Press, Leicester.

Mazzulla, Fred, and Jo Mazzulla

2005   *Brass Checks and Red Lights: Being a Pictorial Pot Pourri of (Historical) Prostitutes, Parlor Houses, Professors, Procuresses, and Pimps.* Fred and Jo Mazzulla, Denver.

McCabe, James D., Jr.

1882   *New York by Sunlight and Gaslight.* Philadelphia. Originally published as Edward Winslow Martin, *The Secrets of the Great City: A Work Descriptive of the Virtues and the Vices, the Mysteries, Miseries, and Crimes of New York City.* National Publishing, 1868.

McGuire, Randall H.

1992   *A Marxist Archaeology.* Academic Press, New York.

Meskell, Lynn

2000   Re-em(bed)ding Sex: Domesticity, Sexuality, and Ritual in New Kingdom Egypt. In *Archaeologies and Sexuality,* edited by Robert A. Schmidt and Barbara L. Voss, 253–262. Routledge, London.

Meyer, Michael D., Erica S. Gibson, and Julia G. Costello

2005   City of Angels, City of Sin: Archaeology in the Los Angeles Red-Light District ca. 1900. *Historical Archaeology* 39(1):107–125.

Miller, George L.

1980   Classification and Economic Scaling of Nineteenth-Century Ceramics. *Historical Archaeology* 14:1–41.

1991   A Revised Set of CC Index Values for Classification and Economic Scaling of English Ceramics from 1787 to 1880. *Historical Archaeology* 25(1):1–25.

Milne, Claudia, and Pamela Crabtree

2001   Prostitutes, a Rabbi, and a Carpenter—Dinner at Five Points in the 1830s. *Historical Archaeology* 35(3):31–48.

Moore, Henrietta L.

2000   Ethics and Ontology: Why Agents and Agency Matter. In *Agency in Archaeology,* edited by Marcia-Anne Dobres and John Robb, pp. 259–263. Routledge, London.

Moran, Rachel

2013   *Paid For: My Journey through Prostitution.* W. W. Norton, New York.

2015   Buying Sex Should Not Be Legal. Op-ed article. *New York Times* 29 August 2015, 19.

Mouer, L. Daniel, Mary Ellen N. Hodges, Stephen R. Potter, Susan L. Henry Renaud, Ivor Noël Hume, Dennis J. Pogue, Martha W. McCartney, and Thomas E. Davidson

1999   Colonoware Pottery, Chesapeake Pipes, and Uncritical Assumptions. In *"I, Too, Am America," Archaeological Studies of African-American Life*, edited by Theresa A. Singleton. University of Virginia Press, Charlottesville.

Mrozowski, Stephen A., James A. Delle, and Robert Paynter

2000   Introduction. In *Lines That Divide: Historical Archaeologies of Race, Class, and Gender*, edited by James A. Delle, Stephen A. Mrozowski, and Robert Paynter, pp. xi–xxxi. University of Tennessee Press, Knoxville.

Mrozowski, Stephen A., Grace H. Ziesing, and Mary C. Beaudry

1996   *Living on the Boott: Historical Archaeology at the Boott Mills Boarding Houses, Lowell, Massachusetts.* University of Massachusetts Press, Amherst.

Munns, Anna M.

2016   The Legal Language of Sex: Interpreting a Hierarchy of Prostitution Using the Terminology of Criminal Charges. Paper presented at the Annual Meeting of the Society for Historical Archaeology, 6–9 January 2016, Washington, DC.

Nassaney, Michael S., and Marjorie R. Abel

2000   Urban Spaces, Labor Organization, and Social Control: Lessons from New England's Nineteenth Century Industry. In *Lines That Divide: Historical Archaeologies of Race, Class, and Gender*, edited by James A. Delle, Stephen A. Mrozowski, and Robert Paynter, pp. 239–275. University of Tennessee Press, Knoxville.

Newman, Richard S.

2008   *Freedom's Prophet: Bishop Richard Allen, the AME Church, and the Black Founding Fathers.* New York University Press, New York.

New York State Census

1855   Census Returns for the Sixth Ward of the City of New York in the County of New York. Manuscript on file, Department of Records and Information, Municipal Archives of the City of New York, 31 Chambers Street, New York.

O'Brien, Elizabeth Barthold

2005   Illicit Congress in the Nation's Capital: The History of Mary Ann Hall's Brothel. *Historical Archaeology* 39(1):47–58.

Orser, Charles E., Jr.

1996   *A Historical Archaeology of the Modern World.* Plenum Press, New York.

2002   Post-processual Archaeology. In *Encyclopedia of Historical Archaeology*, edited by Charles E. Orser, Jr., pp. 444–447. Routledge, New York.

Page, Courtney, and Charles R. Ewen

2016   Recognizing a Pirate Shipwreck without the Skull and Crossbones. In *Pieces of Eight: More Archaeology of Piracy*, edited by Charles R. Ewen and Russell K. Skowronek, pp. 261–273. University Press of Florida, Gainesville.

Paynter, Robert, and Randall H. McGuire

1991   The Archaeology of Inequality: Material Culture, Domination, and Resistance. In *The Archaeology of Inequality*, edited by Randall H. McGuire and Robert Paynter, pp. 1–27. Blackwell, Oxford, UK.

Peiss, Kathy

1986   *Cheap Amusements: Working Women and Leisure in Turn-of-the-Century New York*. Temple University Press, Philadelphia.

1998   *Hope in a Jar: The Making of America's Beauty Culture*. Metropolitan Books, Henry Holt, New York.

Pend d'Oreille News

1892   Big G. *Pend d'Oreille News* 23 April 1(12):3, Sandpoint, Idaho.

Pend d'Oreille Review

1909   Robbed of $200. *Pend d'Oreille Review* 26 November 5(12):1, Sandpoint, Idaho.

Petrich-Guy, Mary

2014   Chapter 4, Appendix II, Absinthe. In *The Other Side of Sandpoint: Early History and Archaeology beside the Tracks*. The Sandpoint Archaeology Project 2006–2013. Vol. 2: *Material Culture of Everyday Life*, edited by Mark S. Warner. SWCA Report No. 14–48. Prepared for Idaho Transportation Department, District 1, Coeur d'Alene, Idaho. SWCA Environmental Consultants, Portland, Oregon.

Petrich-Guy, Mary, Mark S. Warner, and Jamelon Brown

2014   Chapter 4. "Try One of Fatty's 'Velvets'": Drinking and Socializing in Sandpoint. In *The Other Side of Sandpoint: Early History and Archaeology beside the Tracks*. The Sandpoint Archaeology Project 2006–2013. Vol. 2: *Material Culture of Everyday Life*, edited by Mark S. Warner. SWCA Report No. 14–48. Prepared for Idaho Transportation Department, District 1, Coeur d'Alene, Idaho. SWCA Environmental Consultants, Portland, Oregon.

Petrik, Paula

1981   Capitalists with Rooms: Prostitution in Helena, Montana. *Montana* (Spring 1981). Montana Historical Society, Helena.

Pinzer, M. (Maimie)

1977   *The Maimie Papers*, edited by Ruth Rosen. Feminist Press, Old Westbury, New York, in cooperation with the Schlessinger Library of Radcliffe College.

Porter-Lupu, Jennifer

2016   Landscapes of Desire: Mapping the 1880s Brothels of Washington, D.C. Paper presented at the Annual Meeting of the Society for Historical and Underwater Archaeology, Washington, DC.

Prangnell, Jonathan, and Kate Quirk

2009   Children in Paradise: Growing Up on the Australian Goldfields. *Historical Archaeology* 43(3):38–49.

Press, Donald E.

1984   South of the Avenue, from Murder Bay to the Federal Triangle. *Records of the Columbia Historical Society of Washington, D.C.* 51:51–70.

Redfield, Robert
1953   *The Primitive World and Its Transformations*. Cornell University Press, Ithaca.
Reeves, Matthew
2009   Paper presented at the Annual Meeting of the Society for Historical Archaeology, Toronto.
Roberts, Nickie
1992   *Whores in History: Prostitution in Western Society*. Harper-Collins, London.
Rose, Al
1974   *Storyville, New Orleans, Being an Authentic Illustrated Account of the Notorious Red-Light District*. University of Alabama Press, University.
Rosen, Ruth
1982   *The Lost Sisterhood, Prostitution in America, 1900–1918*. Johns Hopkins University Press, Baltimore.
Rothschild, Nan A., and Diana diZerega Wall
2014   *The Archaeology of Cities*. University Press of Florida, Gainesville.
Rotman, Deborah L.
2009   *Historical Archaeology of Gendered Lives*. Springer, New York.
2015   *The Archaeology of Gender in Historic America*. University Press of Florida, Gainesville.
Sachse, E.
1852   *View of Washington*. E. Sachse, Baltimore. Print on file, Prints and Photographs Division, Library of Congress, Washington, DC.
Saitta, Dean J.
2007   *The Archaeology of Collective Action*. University Press of Florida, Gainesville.
Sanborn Map Company
1888   Fire Insurance Map of Washington, D.C. Sanborn Map Company, New York.
1900   Fire Insurance Map of Ouray County, Colorado, Sheet 3. University of Colorado Digital Library Collection.
Sanger, William W.
1939   *The History of Prostitution, Its Extent, Causes, and Effects throughout the World*. New ed. Eugenics Publishing, New York. Originally published 1858.
Schmidt, Peter R., and Stephen A. Mrozowski
1988   Documentary Insights into the Archaeology of Smuggling. In *Documentary Archaeology in the New World*, edited by Mary C. Beaudry, pp. 32–42. Cambridge University Press, Cambridge.
Schmidt, Robert A., and Barbara L. Voss (editors)
2000   *Archaeologies of Sexuality*. Routledge, London.
Seifert, Donna J.
1991   Within Sight of the White House: The Archaeology of Working Women. *Historical Archaeology* 25(4):82–108.
1994   Mrs. Starr's Profession. In *Those of Little Note: Gender Race, and Class in His-*

torical Archaeology, edited by Elizabeth M. Scott, pp. 149–173. University of Arizona Press, Tucson.

Seifert, Donna J., and Joseph Balicki

2005   Mary Ann Hall's House. *Historical Archaeology* 39(1):59–73.

Seifert, Donna J., Joseph Balicki, Elizabeth Barthold O'Brien, Dana B. Heck, Gary McGowan, and Aaron Smith

1998   Archaeological Data Recovery, Smithsonian Institution National Museum of the American Indian, Mall Museum Site. Report submitted to the Smithsonian Institution Office of the Physical Plant and Venturi, Scott Brown and Associates, by John Milner Associates, Inc., Alexandria, Virginia.

Seifert, Donna J., Elizabeth Barthold O'Brien, and Joseph Balicki

2000   Mary Ann Hall's First-Class House: The Archaeology of a Capital Brothel. In *Archaeologies of Sexuality*, edited by Robert A. Schmidt and Barbara L. Voss, pp. 117–128. Routledge, New York.

Shackel, Paul A.

2000   Craft to Wage Labor, Agency and Resistance in American Historical Archaeology. In *Agency in Archaeology*, edited by Marcia-Anne Dobres and John Robb, pp. 232–246. Routledge, London.

2009   *The Archaeology of the American Working Class*. University Press of Florida, Gainesville.

Simmons, Alexy

1982   Red Light Ladies: A Perspective on the Frontier Community. *Northwest Anthropological Research Notes* 16(1):107–114.

1989   Red Light Ladies: Settlement Patterns and Material Culture on the Mining Frontier. *Anthropology Northwest: Number Four*. Department of Anthropology, Oregon State University, Corvallis.

Singleton, Theresa A.

1990   The Archaeology of the Plantation South: A Review of Approaches and Goals. *Historical Archaeology* 24(4):70–77.

Smith, Angela J.

2016   Melvina Massey: Finding and Interpreting Fargo's Most Famous Madam. Paper presented at the Annual Meeting of the Society for Historical Archaeology, 6–9 January 2016, Washington, DC.

Smith-Rosenberg, Carroll

1985   *Disorderly Conduct: Visions of Gender in Victorian America*. Oxford University Press, Oxford.

Snyder, Jeffrey B.

1997   *Romantic Staffordshire Ceramics*. A Schiffer Book for Collectors. Schiffer, Atglen, Pennsylvania.

South, Stanley

1977   *Method and Theory in Historical Archaeology*. Academic Press, New York.

Souvenir Sporting Guide

1964   *Souvenir Sporting Guide.* Reprinted by the Special Collections Department, University of California, Los Angeles. In *Tarnished Angels: Paradisiacal Turpitude in Los Angeles Revealed,* by W. W. Robinson. Originally published in 1897.

Spencer-Wood, Suzanne M. (editor)

1987   *Consumer Choice in Historical Archaeology.* Plenum Press, New York.

1991   Toward an Historical Archaeology of Materialistic Domestic Reform. In *The Archaeology of Inequality,* edited by Randall H. McGuire and Robert Paynter, pp. 231–286. Basil Blackwell, Cambridge, Massachusetts.

Spude, Catherine Holder

2005   Brothels and Saloons: An Archaeology of Gender in the American West. *Historical Archaeology* 39(1):89–106.

Stansell, Christine

1987   *City of Women: Sex and Class in New York, 1789–1860.* University of Illinois Press, Urbana.

Starbuck, David R.

1999   *The Great Warpath: British Military Sites from Albany to Crown Point.* University Press of New England, Hanover, New Hampshire.

State ex rel. Blackall et al. v. Donohue

1843   From research conducted by Timothy Gilfoyle, Loyola University, Chicago.

Steele, Daniel J.

2017   Listening to Voices of the Exploited: Law Enforcement and Sex Trafficking in the United States. In *Challenging Perspectives on Street-Based Sex Work,* edited by Katie Hail-Jares, Corey S. Shdaimah, and Chrysanthi S. Leon, pp. 243–256. Temple University Press, Philadelphia.

Stewart, Susan

1993   *On Longing: Narratives of the Miniature, the Gigantic, the Souvenir, and the Collection.* Duke University Press, Durham, North Carolina.

Storey, John

1998   Postmodernism, Introduction. In *Cultural Theory and Popular Culture: A Reader,* 2nd ed., edited by John Storey, pp. 345–349. University of Georgia Press, Athens.

Strong, Anise K.

2010   Can You Tell Me How to Get to the Roman Brothel? Public Prominence of Prostitutes in the Roman World. Online article based on a doctoral dissertation, Stanford University, June 23, 2010. https://papers.ssrn.com/sol3/papers.cfm?abstract_id=1629314.

Switzer, Ronald R.

1974   *The Bertrand Bottles: A Study of 19th Century Glass and Ceramic Containers.* National Park Service, U.S. Department of the Interior, Washington, DC.

Swords, Molly E., and Breanna Kisling

2014   Come Out, Come Out, Wherever You Are: Seeking Sandpoint's Children. In

The Other Side of Sandpoint: Early History and Archaeology beside the Tracks. The Sandpoint Archaeology Project 2006–2013. Vol. 2: *Material Culture of Everyday Life*, edited by Mark S. Warner. SWCA Report No. 14–48. Prepared for Idaho Transportation Department, District 1, Coeur d'Alene, Idaho. SWCA Environmental Consultants, Portland, Oregon.

Thompson, E. P.

1963   *The Making of the English Working Class.* Victor Gollancz, London.

Tidwell, William A.

1988   *Come Retribution: The Confederate Secret Service and the Assassination of Lincoln.* With James O. Hall and David Winfred Gaddy. University of Mississippi Press, Jackson.

U.S. Army Corps of Engineers (USACE)

1864–1865   Bawdy Houses. Provost Marshal's Department of Washington, 22nd Army Corps. Record Group 393, Vol. 298, National Archives and Records Administration, Washington, DC.

U.S. Bureau of the Census (USBC)

1840   *Manuscript Population Census of the United States, 1840.* Microfilm, National Archives and Records Administration, Washington, DC.

1850   *Manuscript Population Census of the United States, 1850.* Microfilm, National Archives and Records Administration, Washington, DC.

1860   *Manuscript Population Census of the United States, 1860.* Microfilm, National Archives and Records Administration, Washington, DC.

1870   *Manuscript Population Census of the United States, 1870.* Microfilm, National Archives and Records Administration, Washington, DC.

1880   *Manuscript Population Census of the United States, 1880.* Microfilm, National Archives and Records Administration, Washington, DC.

1900   *Manuscript Population Census of the United States, 1900.* Microfilm, National Archives and Records Administration, Washington, DC.

U.S. Congress (USC)

1874   Report of the Joint Select Committee of Congress Appointed to Inquire into the Affairs of the Government of the District of Columbia; Together with the Journal of the Committee, Answer of the Governor, Charges, Arguments, and Testimony. Government Printing Office, Washington, DC.

U.S. vs J. Wilkes Booth

1865   Deposition of Nellie Starr, *United States vs J. Wilkes Booth*, Preliminary Examination, Investigation and Trial Papers Relating to the Assassination of President Lincoln, M-599, reel 6, frame 0258. National Archives and Records Administration, Washington, DC.

Valentine, David T.

1842–1878   *Valentine's Manual of the Municipal Government of the City of New York.* Published annually by David T. Valentine, New York.

Van Buren, Mary, and Kristin A. Gensmer

2017   Crib Girls and Clients in the Red-Light District of Ouray, Colorado: Class, Gender, and Dress. *Historical Archaeology* 51(2):218–239.

Veit, Richard, and Paul W. Schopp

1999   Who's Been Drinking on the Railroad? Archaeological Excavations at the Central Railroad of New Jersey's Lakehurst Shops. *Northeast Historical Archeology* 28:21–40.

Vermeer, Andrea C.

2006   Making the West: Approaches to the Archaeology of Prostitution on the 19th-Century Mining Frontier. Doctoral dissertation, Department of Anthropology, University of Arizona, Tucson.

Walkowitz, Judith R.

1982   *Prostitution and Victorian Society: Women, Class, and the State.* Cambridge University Press, Cambridge.

Wall, Diana diZerega

1991   Sacred Dinners and Secular Teas: Constructing Domesticity in Mid-19th-Century New York. *Historical Archaeology* 25(4):69–81.

1994   *The Archaeology of Gender, Separating the Spheres in Urban America.* Plenum Press, New York.

Warner, Mark S., and James C. Bard

2014   Remembering Trixie Colton: The World of Sandpoint's Prostitutes. In *The Other Side of Sandpoint: Early History and Archaeology beside the Tracks.* The Sandpoint Archaeology Project 2006–2013. Vol. 1: *Sandpoint Stories*, edited by Robert M. Weaver. SWCA Report No. 14-48. Prepared for Idaho Transportation Department, District 1, Coeur d'Alene, Idaho. SWCA Environmental Consultants, Portland, Oregon.

Warner, Mark S., Dan Martin, and Jamelon Brown

2014   The Archaeology of Sex. In *The Other Side of Sandpoint: Early History and Archaeology beside the Tracks.* The Sandpoint Archaeology Project 2006–2013. Vol. 2: *Material Culture of Everyday Life*, edited by Mark S. Warner. SWCA Report No. 14-48. Prepared for Idaho Transportation Department, District 1, Coeur d'Alene, Idaho. SWCA Environmental Consultants, Portland, Oregon.

Wegars, Priscilla

1989   "Inmates of Body Houses": Prostitution in Moscow, Idaho, 1885–1910. *Idaho Yesterdays* 33(1):25–37.

1993   Besides Polly Bemis: Historical and Artefactual Evidence for Chinese Women in the West, 1848–1930. In *Hidden Heritage: Historical Archaeology of the Overseas Chinese*, edited by Priscilla Wegars, pp. 229–254. Baywood, Amityville, New York.

Wilde-Ramsing, Mark

2006   The Pirate Ship *Queen Anne's Revenge*. In *X Marks the Spot: The Archaeology of Piracy*, edited by Russell K. Skowronek and Charles R. Ewen, pp. 160–195. New

Perspectives on Maritime History and Nautical Archaeology, University Press of Florida, Gainesville.

Wilde-Ramsing, Mark U., and Linda F. Carnes-McNaughton

2016   Blackbeard's *Queen Anne's Revenge* and Its French Connection. In *Pieces of Eight: More Archaeology of Piracy,* edited by Charles R. Ewen and Russell K. Skowronek, pp. 15–56. University Press of Florida, Gainesville.

Wilde-Ramsing, Mark U., and Charles R. Ewen

2012   Beyond Reasonable Doubt: A Case for *Queen Anne's Revenge. Historical Archaeology* 46(2):110–133.

Wilkie, Laurie

1997   Secret and Sacred; Contextualizing the Artifacts of African-American Magic and Religion. *Historical Archaeology* 31(4):81–106.

2000   Not Merely Child's Play: Creating a Historical Archaeology of Children and Childhood. In *Children and Material Culture,* edited by Joanna Sofaer Derevenski, 100–113. Routledge, New York.

Within Sight of the White House

[1895] Within Sight of the White House. Unidentified newspaper clipping on file, Geography and Map Division, Library of Congress, Washington, DC.

Wurst, LuAnn, and Robert K. Fitts

1999   Introduction: Why Confront Class? *Historical Archaeology* 33(1):1–6.

Yamin, Rebecca

1998   Lurid Tales and Homely Stories of New York's Notorious Five Points. *Historical Archaeology* 32(1):74–85.

2000   People and Their Possessions. In *Tales of Five Points: Working-Class Life in Nineteenth-Century New York,* 6 vols., edited by Rebecca Yamin. Prepared for Edwards and Kelcy Engineers, Inc. and General Services Administration, Region 2. John Milner Associates, Inc. (now Commonwealth Heritage Group, Inc.), 535 North Church Street, West Chester, Pennsylvania.

2005   Wealthy, Free, and Female: Prostitution in Nineteenth-Century New York. *Historical Archaeology* 39 (1): 4–18.

2008   *Digging in the City of Brotherly Love: Stories from Philadelphia Archaeology.* Yale University Press, New Haven.

2011   Rediscovering Raritan Landing, an Adventure in New Jersey Archaeology. Prepared for the New Jersey Department of Transportation and the Federal Highway Administration.

Yamin, Rebecca (editor)

2000   *Tales of Five Points: Working-Class Life in Nineteenth-Century New York,* 6 vols. Prepared for Edwards and Kelcy Engineers, Inc., and General Services Administration, Region 2. John Milner Associates, Inc. (now Commonwealth Heritage Group, Inc.), 535 North Church Street, West Chester, Pennsylvania.

Yamin, Rebecca, Scott Parker, and Nikki Tobias

2003   Route 18 Section 2A Extension Project, Technical Report No. 1. The Bray/Letson Meadow Property (28-Mi-84). Prepared for Gannett Fleming, Inc., and the New Jersey Department of Transportation. John Milner Associates, Inc.

Yentsch, Anne E., and Mary C. Beaudry

2000   American Material Culture in Mind, Thought, and Deed. In *Archaeological Theory Today*, edited by Ian Hodder, pp. 214–240. Polity Press, Oxford, UK.

Zimmerman, Larry J., and Jessica Welch

2011   Displaced and Barely Visible: Archaeology and the Material Culture of Homelessness. *Historical Archaeology* 45(1):67–85.

Index

Page numbers in *italics* indicate illustrations.

REBECCA YAMIN is a historical archaeologist specializing in urban archaeology. She is retired from John Milner Associates, Inc., where her major projects included the analysis and interpretation of almost a million artifacts recovered on the Five Points site in Lower Manhattan, excavations at the sites of the Independence Visitor Center and Liberty Bell Center on Independence Mall in Philadelphia, and, most recently, at the site of the Museum of the American Revolution. She is the author of *Digging in the City of Brotherly Love: Stories from Philadelphia Archaeology*; *Rediscovering Raritan Landing: An Adventure in New Jersey Archaeology*; and *Excavation at the Site of the Museum of the American Revolution: A Tale of Two Taverns and the Growth of Philadelphia.*

DONNA J. SEIFERT is a registered professional archaeologist specializing in historical archaeology. She managed projects in the Alexandria, Virginia, office of John Milner Associates for 23 years, where she worked on brothel sites in two locations in downtown Washington, DC. She served as the associate editor of *Historical Archaeology* for several years and edited two thematic issues of the journal, Gender in Historical Archaeology (1991) and Sin City (2005). She served as president of the Society for Historical Archaeology in 1995. She now resides in northern New Mexico, where she grows blue corn and green chiles.

The American Experience in Archaeological Perspective

MICHAEL S. NASSANEY, FOUNDING EDITOR

KRYSTA RYZEWSKI, CO-EDITOR

The American Experience in Archaeological Perspective series was established by the University Press of Florida and founding editor Michael S. Nassaney in 2004. This prestigious historical archaeology series focuses attention on a range of significant themes in the development of the modern world from an Americanist perspective. Each volume explores an event, process, setting, institution, or geographic region that played a formative role in the making of the United States of America as a political, social, and cultural entity. These comprehensive overviews underscore the theoretical, methodological, and substantive contributions that archaeology has made to the study of American history and culture. Rather than subscribing to American exceptionalism, the authors aim to illuminate the distinctive character of the American experience in time and space. While these studies focus on historical archaeology in the United States, they are also broadly applicable to historical and anthropological inquiries in other parts of the world. To date the series has produced more than two dozen titles. Prospective authors are encouraged to contact the Series Editors to learn more.

The Archaeology of Collective Action, by Dean J. Saitta (2007)

The Archaeology of Institutional Confinement, by Eleanor Conlin Casella (2007)

The Archaeology of Race and Racialization in Historic America, by Charles E. Orser Jr. (2007)

The Archaeology of North American Farmsteads, by Mark D. Groover (2008)

The Archaeology of Alcohol and Drinking, by Frederick H. Smith (2008)

The Archaeology of American Labor and Working-Class Life, by Paul A. Shackel (2009; first paperback edition, 2011)

The Archaeology of Clothing and Bodily Adornment in Colonial America, by Diana DiPaolo Loren (2010; first paperback edition, 2011)

The Archaeology of American Capitalism, by Christopher N. Matthews (2010; first paperback edition, 2012)

The Archaeology of Forts and Battlefields, by David R. Starbuck (2011; first paperback edition, 2012)

The Archaeology of Consumer Culture, by Paul R. Mullins (2011; first paperback edition, 2012)

The Archaeology of Antislavery Resistance, by Terrance M. Weik (2012; first paperback edition, 2013)

The Archaeology of Citizenship, by Stacey Lynn Camp (2013; first paperback edition, 2019)

The Archaeology of American Cities, by Nan A. Rothschild and Diana diZerega Wall (2014; first paperback edition, 2015)

The Archaeology of American Cemeteries and Gravemarkers, by Sherene Baugher and Richard F. Veit (2014; first paperback edition, 2015)

The Archaeology of Smoking and Tobacco, by Georgia L. Fox (2015; first paperback edition, 2016)

The Archaeology of Gender in Historic America, by Deborah L. Rotman (2015; first paperback edition, 2018)

The Archaeology of the North American Fur Trade, by Michael S. Nassaney (2015; first paperback edition, 2017)

The Archaeology of the Cold War, by Todd A. Hanson (2016; first paperback edition, 2019)

The Archaeology of American Mining, by Paul J. White (2017; first paperback edition, 2020)

The Archaeology of Utopian and Intentional Communities, by Stacy C. Kozakavich (2017; first paperback edition, 2023)

The Archaeology of American Childhood and Adolescence, by Jane Eva Baxter (2019)

The Archaeology of Northern Slavery and Freedom, by James A. Delle (2019)

The Archaeology of Prostitution and Clandestine Pursuits, by Rebecca Yamin and Donna J. Seifert (2019; first paperback edition, 2023)

The Archaeology of Southeastern Native American Landscapes of the Colonial Era, by Charles R. Cobb (2019)

The Archaeology of the Logging Industry, by John G. Franzen (2020)

The Archaeology of Craft and Industry, by Christopher C. Fennell (2021)

The Archaeology of the Homed and the Unhomed, by Daniel O. Sayers (2023)

CPSIA information can be obtained
at www.ICGtesting.com
Printed in the USA
JSHW070030051222
34157JS00004B/13